TEAM BUILDING: One Hour Workshop

Carol A. Silvis, M.Ed.

Cengage Learning PTR

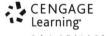

CENGAGE
Learning·

Professional · Technical · Reference

Australia, Brazil, Japan, Korea, Mexico, Singapore, Spain, United Kingdom, United States

CENGAGE Learning
Professional • Technical • Reference

Team Building:
One Hour Workshop
Carol A. Silvis, M.Ed.

Publisher and General Manager,
Cengage Learning PTR:
Stacy L. Hiquet

Manager of Editorial Services:
Heather Talbot

Senior Product Manager:
Mitzi Koontz

Project and Copy Editor:
Karen A. Gill

Interior Layout:
Shawn Morningstar

Cover Designer:
Luke Fletcher

Proofreader:
Jenny Davidson

For product information and technology assistance, contact us at
Cengage Learning Customer & Sales Support, 1-800-354-9706.

For permission to use material from this text or product,
submit all requests online at **cengage.com/permissions.**

Further permissions questions can be emailed to
permissionrequest@cengage.com.

All trademarks are the property of their respective owners.

Library of Congress Control Number: 2015934728

ISBN-13: 978-1-305-50991-7

ISBN-10: 1-305-50991-9

Cengage Learning PTR
20 Channel Center Street
Boston, MA 02210
USA

Cengage Learning is a leading provider of customized learning solutions with office locations around the globe, including Singapore, the United Kingdom, Australia, Mexico, Brazil, and Japan. Locate your local office at: **international.cengage.com/region.**

Cengage Learning products are represented in Canada by Nelson Education, Ltd.

For your lifelong learning solutions, visit **cengageptr.com.**

Visit our corporate website at **cengage.com.**

Printed in the United States of America
Print Number: 01   Print Year: 2015

This book is dedicated to my family, Ryan, Niki, and Mikaila,
who encourage and inspire me every day.

Acknowledgments

A special thanks to Mitzi Koontz, senior product manager, for her vision and support with this project, and to Karen Gill, project and copy editor, for her expertise and assistance. It is a pleasure to work with such dedicated professionals. Thanks also to the many others who had a hand in producing this book.

About the Author

Carol A. Silvis, M.Ed., is the author of *Presentation Skills: One Hour Workshop*; *101 Ways to Connect with Customers, Chiefs, and Coworkers*; *Job Hunting After 50*; *101 Ways to Make Yourself Indispensable at Work*; and *100% Externship Success and General Office Procedures*, all available through Cengage Learning. Other publications include "Time Management and Organization for Writers" (2012 *Writers Market*), a dozen creative nonfiction stories and inspirational pieces published in national magazines, and more than 40 articles published in various newsletters.

Carol has been interviewed for Yahoo.com, AARP online, CBSMoneywatch.com, ABCNews.com, and *Writer's Digest*; she has also appeared on Cornerstone TV, HMC-TV, and WIUP-TV.

She has a master's in education and has trained adults in how to get a job, keep and enjoy it, and get ahead. She gives workshops and seminars for schools, businesses, professional organizations, and libraries on a wide range of business topics.

Carol is the president of Pennwriters, Inc., coordinating her third conference. In 2008, she received the Meritorious Service Award.

Visit her website at www.carolsilvis.com and her blog at www.carolsilvis.blogspot.com.

Table of Contents

Introduction viii

Part I Creating Successful Teams

Chapter 1 Creating Successful Teams   1

Teams Versus Individuals 2
Benefits of a Team 4
Factors That Promote Success. 6
Character Traits of Successful Team Members. 7
Trust and Commitment 9
Team Support. 9
Team Performance 12
Team Meetings. 13
Communication. 14

Chapter 2 Organizing the Team   17

Determine the Team's Purpose 18
Clarify the Purpose. 19
Decide on the Size of the Team 19
Decide the Team Structure. 19
Select the Team Members 20
Inspire the Team. 22
Manage the Team. 22
Set the Policies and Procedures. 22
Hold Team Members Accountable 24
Provide Resources. 25
Restructure the Team 27

Chapter 3 Setting Team Roles and Goals   29

Defining Goals. 30
Setting Team Goals. 31
Roles 37

Part II Understanding and Motivating Team Members

Chapter 4 Considering Culture, Competition, Cooperation, and Communication   39

Culture. 39
Competition 42
Cooperation. 43
Communication. 45

Chapter 5 Motivating Team Members   49

Motivation 49
Visualize. 54
Commitment 55
Affirmations 57
Challenges 58

Part III Managing Teams

Chapter 6 Filling the Leader/Facilitator Role   59

Defining Leaders 59
Assessing Leadership Skills 60
Monitoring the Team 62
Increasing Productivity. 64
Providing Feedback 65
Making Decisions 66
Sharing the Vision 66

Chapter 7 Making Group Decisions and Negotiating   69

Building Trust 69
Building Rapport 71
Accepting Accountability 72
Negotiating with the Team 73

Chapter 8 Solving Problems   77

Identifying Problems 77
Analyzing Problems 78
Thinking Critically. 79

Creating Solutions 80
Determining the Appropriate Solution. 82
Implementing the Solution 82

Chapter 9 Handling Conflict   85

Identifying Sources of Conflict. 85
Managing Conflict. 87
Passing Blame. 89
Collaborating. 90
Using Demographics 91
Addressing the Problems 92

Chapter 10 Empowering Teams   93

Establishing an Environment for Success 93
Leading the Empowered Team 94
Energizing Team Members. 96
Assessing Empowered Team Members 97
Building Self-Esteem 99

Chapter 11 Using Team Building Exercises   101

Using Icebreakers 102
Reenergizing Team Members 103
Pitting Teams Against Each Other 103

Introduction

The suggestions in this book will guide those who organize or work in teams. This book will benefit people who want to become better team leaders, team members, and teammates.

Companies rely on teams to work together to solve problems, analyze results, implement new technologies, and the like. Those teams can only be successful to the extent they pull together to complete tasks, arrive at plausible conclusions, and implement their ideas.

Team players must be able to connect with and get along with others. They must put the team goals above their own agendas. They must be experts in their fields with highly developed skills.

Employees who strive to become valuable team members must continually strive to do and be their best. As a result, they will be invaluable to their organizations.

How This Book Is Organized

This book provides team building tips and guidelines as well as exercises and checklists to help you put the ideas you read about into practice. Chapter 1, "Creating Successful Teams," discusses the importance of using teams to get more done. Chapter 2, "Organizing the Team," gives pointers for assembling a team geared toward success. Chapter 3, "Setting Team Roles and Goals," provides guidelines for determining the roles for each team member based on his or her expertise and skills. Chapter 4, "Considering Culture, Competition, Cooperation, and Communication," provides tips to help team members become a cohesive group. Chapter 5, "Motivating Team Members," recommends ways to encourage team members to motivate themselves and others. Chapter 6, "Filling the Leader/Facilitator Role," stresses the importance of having the right leadership to guide team members toward the team's goals. Chapter 7, "Making Group Decisions and Negotiating," suggests ways to make better decisions. Chapter 8, "Solving Problems," provides tips for analyzing and solving problems. Chapter 9, "Handling Conflict," stresses the importance of team members working together to reach the team's goals. Chapter 10, "Empowering Teams," recommends ways to empower team members. Chapter 11, "Using Team Building Exercises," provides several team building activities.

Who This Book Is For

This book will benefit people who hope to become successful team players. The information presented is intended for employees who are just starting out and for those who want to improve their team building skills.

1 Creating Successful Teams

Teams are widely used in companies and organizations as vehicles for attaining goals and completing tasks. The theory is that a team of people is more effective than individuals working alone. Teams are not always the answer to reaching an organization's goals, but there is something to be said for people working together and sharing their expertise. Employers who believe more can be achieved with several employees tackling issues jointly rather than as individuals may prefer to leverage teams to get the job done.

Groups of people working together do not necessarily make a team. A team is assembled for a specific mission, and its members fully commit to the team goals, work together to accomplish them, and hold one another accountable until the goals are attained.

Teams provide an opportunity to link employees who have diverse views, knowledge, and skills and use these talents to complete projects, solve problems, increase quality, learn to get along with one another, attain goals, and any number of other issues.

To build a team successfully, you will not want to combine just any group of employees and give them a job to do. Building an effective team takes time, commitment, and thoughtful planning.

Begin by identifying your needs and the expertise and skills required to resolve them. Then choose the team members accordingly.

1

TEAMS VERSUS INDIVIDUALS

Employers place a lot of weight on individual performance, expertise, and skills, but many also rely on teams. Should you use a team in your workplace? Although individuals can perform most tasks successfully, employees must learn to work together for the good of the company and its customers. Teams offer a means of bringing people together to share knowledge, ideas, values, responsibility, skills, and commitment.

Many employees are accustomed to performing as individuals and prefer it that way. They like single-handedly accomplishing tasks and the rewards and accolades associated with their individual achievement. Some of them lack the social skills necessary to work well with others. A team may not bring out these employees' best qualities unless you help them develop their interpersonal skills and convince them of the value of a job well done as a team member.

Teams have been used in companies for years and can be effective for improving everything from products and services to employee performance and morale. However, teams are not always effective or successful in attaining their goals. If the team fails to reach its goals, the team members can still take away something positive from the experience if they are willing to learn from their mistakes.

You will want to weigh the pros and cons before assembling a team. Some company goals and objectives may be better handled by a team for a number of reasons, including the following:

- The organization is expanding rapidly.
- Productivity is decreasing among employees.
- Conflicts plague employees.
- The organization appears fragmented.
- The organization has a difficult problem to solve.
- The organization has a special project to complete.
- Tasks are not carried out properly.
- A variety of options for handling tasks is wanted.
- Discrimination complaints have surfaced.
- Products are of poor quality.
- Customer service needs to be improved.
- The organization wants to increase profits.
- The organization plans to have employees share thinking.
- The organization plans to have employees share their knowledge and skills.
- The organization requires employees to work together.

Any of the preceding factors, as well as other reasons, could necessitate creating teams. The specific problem an organization hopes to address will determine what type of team structure is required, such as a permanent work team, a one-time project team, a fact-finding team, an assessment team, and so forth. Chapter 2, "Organizing the Team," provides more information on how to assemble a team.

Exercise: Assess Your Organization's Needs

Assess your particular organization's needs to gain a better grasp of whether you (or the organization) should consider forming teams among your employees. Write your answers here.

What are the particular issues of the organization that you feel require a team response? _____

_____

_____

_____

How can using a team help fulfill the above? _____

_____

_____

_____

_____

What team structure would best suit these needs? _____

_____

What team member roles are necessary to address these needs? _____

_____

_____

_____

What team and individual goals would best support the team in resolving the issue at hand? _____

_____

_____

_____

What resources are available to support a team that is addressing the needs you have identified? _____

_____

_____

_____

BENEFITS OF A TEAM

If any or all of the reasons in the preceding list pertain to your organization, you might feel that creating teams would be an appropriate practice in your workplace. If so, you may ask, "What benefits can my organization expect to receive from creating teams rather than assigning tasks to individuals?"

That question is difficult to answer because what might benefit one organization in a particular situation may not benefit another in the same type of situation. In addition, as mentioned earlier, not all teams are successful in completing their assignments or reaching their goals. For those teams that achieve success, the rewards for the individuals involved and for the organization as a whole can be satisfying and extremely valuable.

Benefits that individuals may receive from working on a team are numerous, including reduced workload, shared vision and responsibilities, exposure to diverse backgrounds and views, and the like. An individual has limited skills and experience, but working on a team allows him to share in other team members' experiences, learn skills, and gain knowledge from them.

Teams also provide support that an individual alone would not receive. Team members may take more risks because of this support and encouragement. Teamwork also offers a greater opportunity to catch mistakes because of multiple members reviewing the work.

Assuming a team you assemble will be successful, your organization can expect to reap one or more of the following benefits:

- ✦ Increased brainstorming and problem-solving ability
- ✦ Expanded idea base
- ✦ Established alliance among team members
- ✦ Developed cooperation among team members and other employees
- ✦ Improved quality control
- ✦ Shared knowledge and skills
- ✦ Cross-trained employees
- ✦ Committed team members, leading to enhanced performance
- ✦ Upgraded procedures
- ✦ Achieved goals
- ✦ Completed projects
- ✦ Sharpened negotiating skills among team members
- ✦ Advanced decision-making skills
- ✦ Expanded range of experiences
- ✦ Added support from other members
- ✦ Enhanced creativity among team members
- ✦ Honed interpersonal skills among team members
- ✦ Leveraged strengths and talents among team members
- ✦ Combined resources

- ✦ Diversified values, interests, and ideas
- ✦ Empowered employees
- ✦ Shared vision and purpose
- ✦ Reduced workload on individuals
- ✦ Shared responsibility for failures
- ✦ Increased ability to catch mistakes
- ✦ Improved communication skills
- ✦ Enriched understanding between employees and customers

As you can see, there are definite advantages to using teams. Your organization's benefits may differ from those just explained, or you may gain additional benefits depending on your particular requirements and how the team has met those needs. At the very least, a successful team will complete the goals set for it.

Exercise: Assess the Benefits of Using a Team

Think about a problem or a need that your organization or department has right now and answer the following questions.

Do you feel your organization could benefit from using a team to solve this problem or fill this need? Why or why not?_____

_____

_____

_____

_____

_____

_____

What would be the benefits of using a team rather than an individual to solve this problem or meet this need?

_____

_____

_____

_____

_____

FACTORS THAT PROMOTE SUCCESS

A number of factors can increase or decrease the chances that a team will succeed. Many of these factors are discussed throughout this book. There is no one-size-fits-all approach for putting together a team or guaranteeing its success. However, there are things you can do to create a winning team, and you should make every effort toward that end.

Set and convey the ground rules for team participants. Clearly communicate the goals of the team, the timeframe for completing them, and the resources available to assist the team. Let the team members know where their efforts will contribute to the overall organization. Determine team members' roles and responsibilities. Tell team members how their progress will be measured and reported.

Choosing the right team members is critical to success, as is forming the right sized team and the appropriate structure, defining the purpose for creating the team, listing the team and individual goals, proposing the team management, and compiling the available resources. Chapter 2 provides further guidelines for putting the team together.

Take the necessary time to plan before creating your team. Think about what your organization needs and how to go about addressing those needs. Consider who the best people would be to accomplish the organization's goals and the process these individuals would employ.

Factors that contribute to creating a successful team include, but are not limited to, the following:

+ A suitable, acceptable team purpose
+ The size of the team
+ Adequate resources available to the team, such as money, time, supplies, information, experts, skilled workers, training, and the like
+ Clearly defined goals for individuals and for the team
+ Clearly defined team member roles
+ Reasonable deadlines
+ Procedures and policies for the team
+ Competent team leadership
+ A conflict-management policy
+ Synergy among team members
+ A shared team vision
+ Agreed-upon team goals from the outset
+ Open communication among team members
+ Open communication with the entire company
+ Trust among team members
+ Collaborative team members who are willing to compromise for the good of the team even if they are not in agreement with decisions

- ✦ Team members who hold themselves accountable for attaining their individual goals and those of the team
- ✦ Flexible and open-minded team members
- ✦ Knowledgeable, skilled team members
- ✦ Team members who are willingly to share their knowledge and skills
- ✦ Team members who encourage and support one another
- ✦ Team members who are dedicated to the team
- ✦ Team members who are motivated

Scanning the preceding list, you can see how important it is for team members to possess a number of positive character traits.

CHARACTER TRAITS OF SUCCESSFUL TEAM MEMBERS

Choosing the right team members greatly increases team success. As indicated in the list in the previous section, team members must exhibit character traits conducive to working cooperatively with others. Basic traits such as trust, cooperation, motivation, flexibility, dedication, accountability, knowledge, and the like promote success.

To be successful, the team must consist of members who are able to put aside their individualistic thinking and fully commit to the team's goals. Otherwise, discussions may turn into a test of wills, and problem-solving opportunities will be lost.

The ideal team members will show a commitment to the team goals and will complete their individual tasks as assigned. They should be able to contribute to the development of a process for attaining the team goals. Additionally, they will monitor their progress as well as that of all team members and hold themselves and others accountable for performing the tasks assigned.

Supportive team members are trustworthy and cooperative. They keep their word, complete their responsibilities, and keep their team members informed of progress. They work to develop a positive relationship with teammates.

Although team members must have positive character traits, additional consideration must be given to the tasks to be completed and the roles to be filled. Successful teams choose individuals who fit the criteria for fulfilling the team's goals. For instance, if the goal includes developing a budget for an upcoming event, select a team member who has a financial background or experience with budgeting. Ask yourself these questions: Who will bring the best perspective to the situation the team faces? Who has the expertise to carry out the tasks required to attain the goal? Who has the necessary skills to do the job?

If you are in a position in which you must choose team members, the guidelines in Chapter 2 will provide helpful hints to assist you.

Assess your positive character traits by completing the following checklist.

Positive Character Traits Checklist	Exhibit	Hope to Improve	Do Not Exhibit
Responsive			
Positive			
Enthusiastic			
Trustworthy			
Dependable			
Flexible			
Efficient			
Cooperative			
Skilled			
Knowledgeable			
Committed			
Motivated			
Creative			
Self-disciplined			
Open-minded			
Supportive			
Tactful			
Considerate			
Helpful			
Respectful			
Proactive			
Accountable			

You should have indicated you exhibit these personal traits. Work toward correcting any traits you do not possess or that you hope to improve.

Exercise: Describe the Type of Team Member with Whom You Would Like to Work

Make a list of personal character traits you would like to see in members of your team.

_____

_____

_____

_____

_____

_____

TRUST AND COMMITMENT

Team members must be committed to seeing the team's goals through to fruition. Otherwise, they will not work with diligence and efficiency. Build commitment by letting people know exactly what is expected of them and to what degree they must perform their assigned tasks. Tell them the details upfront so there is no confusion later. Help them see how much their contributions and the quality of their work matters.

If you are creating and leading a team, make sure everyone on the team knows the level of your commitment to them and to the team's goals. Let team members know what they can expect from you and what you expect from them. Hold yourself and everyone else on the team accountable.

Build trust with teammates by letting them know you are interested in them and want them to succeed. Always be honest, and help them whenever you can. Communicate your feelings and encourage them to do the same. Give every individual credit when due. Fulfill your obligations to teammates and to the team in a timely manner. When you say you will do something, make sure you follow through.

Follow the procedures established for sharing information. If the team discusses restricted information that should stay among team members, keep the information confidential. Know what you can and cannot tell other employees about the team and its decisions.

TEAM SUPPORT

If you are called on to work on a team, be an asset. What will you bring to the team? What are your personal traits, skills, knowledge, and resources?

You must exhibit positive character traits that will move the team forward, including enthusiasm and efficiency. Hold yourself accountable to complete your tasks efficiently. Be willing to do your part to reach the team's goals and meet deadlines.

Share your knowledge, ideas, and skills with team members. Learn and grow from their expertise. Be flexible and open-minded.

Get along with other team members and treat them with respect. Put your best foot forward when participating in discussions. Disagree without being destructive or restricting your teammates' creativity. Always keep the team's goals in mind.

Your teammates will bring their own values, knowledge, skills, and uniqueness to the team. Take advantage of their expertise by learning all you can from them.

Complete the following checklist the next time you are called on to work on a team.

	Yes	No
I have an agreeable personality.		
I am motivated.		
I am fully committed to the team.		
I hold myself accountable to completing tasks assigned to me by the team.		
I complete tasks correctly and to the best of my ability.		
I meet deadlines.		
I compromise when it is for the good of the team.		
I trust my teammates.		
My teammates can trust me.		
I respect my teammates.		
I participate in team discussions.		
I get along with others.		
I willingly share my knowledge and skills with my teammates.		
I am flexible.		
I am open-minded.		
I encourage and support my teammates.		
I share the organization's vision.		
I act in a professional manner at all times when dealing with my teammates.		

You should have answered yes to each item in the checklist. Work toward correcting any negative answers.

Exercise: Determine How You Will Improve

List your personal character traits that could use improvement and the subsequent steps you can take to accomplish the improvement.

Character trait _____

Steps to improve _____

_____

_____

Character trait _____

Steps to improve _____

_____

_____

Character trait _____

Steps to improve _____

_____

_____

Character trait _____

Steps to improve _____

_____

_____

Exercise: Determine What You Will Bring to the Team

These are the specific things I will bring to the team to move it closer to its goal:

_____

_____

_____

_____

_____

_____

_____

_____

TEAM PERFORMANCE

Every team member must exert effort to reach the team's goals. To begin with, members must be clear on what is expected of them. The team leader must establish clear expectations for each individual on the team, including roles and goals. The leader must also state the consequences of not fulfilling obligations.

Team performance should be monitored to keep abreast of whether team members are effective in completing their tasks and meeting deadlines. Who will be in charge of monitoring the group? If a team member is not performing at optimum levels, it's important to take immediate steps to remedy the situation. Who will approach the under-performing employee? Chapter 6, "Filling the Leader/Facilitator Role," discusses overseeing and monitoring team members.

Team member collaboration has a huge bearing on the team's success. Explore ways to develop rapport among team members. When team members share commonalities, trust and cooperation come easier. Everyone should treat his teammate with respect and consideration at all times.

Members who stir up dissatisfaction and conflict are detrimental to the team's reaching its goals. Therefore, if at all possible, select members who are likely to get along and promote the team's goals. Tips for dealing with disgruntled team members are discussed in Chapter 9, "Handling Conflict."

Exercise: Determine Outcomes

Think about the following situations and decide how you would handle each of them.

A teammate has not completed the assignment she was to bring to the meeting.

_____

_____

_____

_____

A teammate complains about every task she is asked to complete.

_____

_____

_____

_____

A teammate disagrees with every idea that a certain other teammate proposes.

_____

_____

_____

_____

You do not like the task you have been given to complete for the team.

_____

_____

_____

_____

TEAM MEETINGS

Meetings provide an opportunity to discuss goals and ideas, work on tasks, share information and skills, review progress, set new goals, change roles or tasks, and so forth. Team members must meet on a regular basis if they are to form a cohesive, effective team. If teams do not hold regular meetings, the members are essentially acting as individuals, not as a team.

Develop a schedule for the initial meeting and distribute it to all team members well in advance. As each meeting concludes, make plans to set the date, time, and place for the next meeting. The frequency of the meetings depends on the needs of the members.

The following are some questions related to meetings that must be answered:

- Why are team meetings necessary?
- How often will the team meet?
- Where and when will the team meet?
- What time will the meeting start, and approximately how long will it last?
- Who will lead the meeting?
- What is the meeting's agenda?
- Who will decide what is on the agenda?
- How much time will be devoted to agenda items?
- What are the consequences if team members are late to meetings?
- What are the consequences if team members miss a meeting?
- What are the consequences if team members come to the meeting unprepared or have not completed their tasks?
- How will team members who miss meetings get caught up on the team's progress, decisions, ideas, and so forth?
- Who will be assigned the task of catching up team members who miss meetings?
- Who will be assigned the task of carrying out consequences against under-performing team members?

Meetings can take up a considerable amount of time, and team members will likely have other responsibilities besides those of the team. They may have to be shown the value of taking time out of their normal work schedules to meet with team members on a regular basis. Make it clear to everyone involved what they are working toward and the reason the team's goals are important to the overall success of the organization.

At the first meeting, introduce all members, establish rules of behavior, define individual roles, assign individual tasks, develop procedures, and explain how everything and everyone works for the greater good of the organization.

To ensure meetings do not end up being a waste of everyone's time, be prompt and encourage every member to be prompt. The meeting should start on time even if someone is late. Delaying the meeting will encourage the late member and every other member to adhere to the bad habit. A late start also inconveniences everyone who must stick to daily schedules.

Assign someone to prepare an agenda for the meeting. This could be the team leader or a person who has been appointed to run the meetings. Send the meeting agenda ahead of time so team members have time to review it and prepare for what they need to bring to the meeting. List the approximate time allotted for each item on the agenda.

COMMUNICATION

Open lines of communication among team members and between the team and the person who created the team and with the organization as a whole are paramount to success. Communication is discussed in detail in Chapter 4, "Considering Culture, Competition, Cooperation, and Communication."

Exercise: Determine Outcomes

In your opinion, are the meetings you are usually asked to attend important and worthwhile? Why or why not? _____

_____

_____

_____

_____

_____

_____

How can you improve meetings you are required to hold? _____

_____

_____

_____

_____

_____

_____

Tips for Team Success

✦   Clearly convey the purpose for assembling a team.

✦   Choose appropriate team members.

✦   Limit the size of the team.

✦   Build rapport and trust among team members.

✦   Encourage cooperation and collaboration among team members.

✦   Clearly define and convey the team's goals.

✦   Assign individual roles.

✦   Assign individual and team goals.

✦   Decide on team leadership.

✦   Inspire the team.

✦   Define the policies and procedures governing the team.

✦   Keep the lines of communication open.

✦   Monitor the progress of the team.

2 Organizing the Team

Teams might be created for a number of reasons, from performing daily tasks to completing one-time projects. Therefore, teams follow different structures and have various numbers of members, depending on the reason the team has been organized and the particular task(s) assigned to the team members. For instance, if an organization wants to plan an employee picnic, a team of two or three people might be sufficient. If the organization wants to improve customer service, it may want several members and a mix of management and front-end employees on the team.

The organizers of a team should think about why it would be in the best interest of the company to assemble a team in the first place. Then they should plan a strategy for putting together a winning team.

DETERMINE THE TEAM'S PURPOSE

Spend some time thinking about the organization's purpose for creating a team. This purpose or team vision must be important enough to convince team members to support it. After all, they must commit time from their regular schedules to attend team meetings and perform tasks necessary to reach the team goals.

Having a strong sense of purpose will assist you in choosing the structure of the team and in securing members whose backgrounds meet desired criteria. Be specific when defining the purpose. Rather than say, "We want to improve customer service," say, "Customer complaints have risen 20 percent this year. Let's find out the reasons behind these complaints and figure out how we can decrease them by 10 percent in the future."

Here are some questions to take into consideration when defining the purpose for creating a team:

- ✦ Does the organization need team members to complete daily tasks, such as quality control or customer service?

- ✦ Does the organization have a special project a team needs to tackle?

- ✦ Does the organization have a complex issue to resolve?

- ✦ Does the organization have a need for specialized expertise?

- ✦ Does the organization have an ongoing function that specific experts need to perform?

- ✦ Does the organization hope to build camaraderie?

- ✦ Is there a change in corporate structure?

- ✦ Does the organization need to coordinate the work of different departments?

- ✦ Will it require several people to fulfill the desired purpose?

- ✦ Will teams be used throughout the organization or in a specific department?

- ✦ Is it likely that team members will support the desired purpose?

- ✦ What impact will the desired purpose have on the entire organization?

Exercise: Establish the Team's Purpose

The next time you are called upon to lead a team or to work on a team, clearly state the team's purpose and then take the following steps:

- ✦ If the team's purpose is unclear, help the team clarify it.

- ✦ If you are not the team's leader, restate the purpose as you understand it and ask if you have interpreted the purpose correctly.

- ✦ If you are the leader, ask your team members to restate the team's purpose to you to determine if they correctly understand it.

CLARIFY THE PURPOSE

Once the purpose is defined by the person or organization calling for a team, it must be made crystal clear to the person establishing the team, the team leader, and all the team members. A breakdown in defining the purpose could have a dramatic negative effect on the success of the team.

The team leader must be able to clearly and succinctly convey the team purpose to its members. When the leader does not fully comprehend the purpose, she will not be able to convey it to the team in a way members will understand. If team members do not understand the purpose, they may be ill prepared to address it properly. In addition, they may not believe in the purpose or want to undertake the tasks necessary to reach the team goals.

Team leaders and members must have good communication skills. Chapter 4, "Considering Culture, Competition, Cooperation, and Communication," provides tips for keeping the lines of communication open.

DECIDE ON THE SIZE OF THE TEAM

Once you decide the purpose for creating a team, you need to determine how many people are required to perform the necessary tasks to attain the goals. Contain the team to a number appropriate for your objectives. For example, if you are putting together a series of workshops for employee training, you can probably do with two or three team members. If you are determining the best way to increase customer satisfaction, you may need six or seven individuals.

Try to keep the size of the team manageable—ideally a dozen or fewer members. If you bring too many people together, you may end up defeating your purpose. The team could wind up in endless discussions or scattered efforts. Larger teams tend to spend more time in discussions, delay decision-making, and have a harder time forming a cohesive group. It is better to break a large team, such as one made of an entire department, into smaller teams.

Small teams tend to be better at accomplishing tasks and arriving at decisions in a timely manner, so long as they are composed of the right people. A small number of experts with the right skills who understand the team's vision and are committed and willing to hold themselves accountable for attaining the team's goals increase the team's chances of success. Small teams are also easier to monitor than large ones.

DECIDE THE TEAM STRUCTURE

Team structure varies according to the purpose and size of the team, how the team and its goals will aid the organization, the work that needs to be done, who will do the work, and who will manage the team.

Types of teams include those that perform daily work, that are designed to work on a special project, that address a significant problem, and so forth.

One consideration for the team is deciding where the power lies. Who will manage the team? Small teams of two or three people might direct themselves without answering to a specific leader. The person who directed the formation of the team may assign another team's manager, or team members may choose this person. Still other teams may be self-governing.

Regardless of how the team is led, the team must have a purpose, goals, procedures to follow, a plan for monitoring progress, and consequences for not meeting goals. Other considerations are deciding what needs to be done, how the work should be performed, and who should perform it. Someone must make all these decisions and implement them. The same person may or may not perform all these tasks.

SELECT THE TEAM MEMBERS

You want to select the best team members available that fit your purpose because these individuals have a strong impact on the success of the team. Even with the best planning, not all teams are successful; however, chances are greatly improved with the right people.

You should choose team members based on a combination of skills, knowledge, and personal traits, not on things like their titles or a close proximity to each other in the workplace. Although occupying offices next to each other could make working together convenient, the individuals may not create the best team.

Organizers should strive to find individuals who will understand the overall team goals and who have the expertise and skills necessary to reach those goals. These individuals should also understand the implications of both attaining and failing to attain the team goals. They must hold themselves accountable, be willing to forgo individual recognition for the good of the team, and possess positive character traits.

The person tasked with organizing a specific team has many questions to consider to come up with the right mix of team members. Here are some questions to ask yourself if you are choosing team members:

- Why is the team being organized?
- Who will select the team members?
- How many people should be on the team?
- In what way are the individual team members expected to contribute to the team?
- Are the individuals being considered likely to get along with each other?
- What type of skills and knowledge are required of the members?
- Do the individuals being considered have skills that complement one another?
- Do the individuals being considered have positive personal traits?
- Will a leader or facilitator be chosen, will the team choose the leader, or will the leadership be shared among members?
- What are the intended goals of the team?
- How should the work be divided among team members?
- Who should divide and assign the work?
- How long will the team have to complete its goals?
- Will the team have access to necessary resources to complete its goals?
- Will the team work with other teams?

As you can see from the preceding list, there is a lot to consider if you want to build the right team. It is not just a matter of telling a few people to work together.

On occasion, you may have to choose a team member who does not possess acceptable character traits but has critical knowledge or skills to contribute to the team goals. In such a case, the team leader should let the person know why she was chosen and why it's important to do whatever it takes to reach the team goals. The team leader should also monitor the person's progress toward achieving team goals and communicate the consequences of negative behavior. Otherwise, you could be setting your team up for unnecessary conflict and aggravation for no good reason.

Get Organized	Yes	No
I know the team's mission.		
I know the team's goals.		
I know what the team needs to do to reach the goals.		
I know when the team goals must be met.		
I know (or am) the team leader.		
I know my role within the team.		
I know how work will be divided.		
I know what my specific duties are.		
I know how to complete my duties.		
I know the date when my duties must be completed.		
I know how the team will be evaluated to determine if goals are met.		
I know the consequences if my individual goals are not met.		
I know the consequences if the team goals are not met.		

You should have answered yes to each item in the checklist. Work toward correcting any negative answers.

Exercise: Choose the Team

Create a list of criteria you would use to choose a team. _____

_____

_____

_____

_____

_____

INSPIRE THE TEAM

The purpose for creating a team may not always impassion every member of the team. This lack of enthusiasm affects the entire team. It is the responsibility of the team's leader to inspire everyone and get him to see how the team's purpose will contribute to the organization's success.

People who do not feel they have anything to contribute to the team's purpose, who do not want to do the tasks assigned, who do not get along with the other people chosen for the team, and the like, will not be good candidates for the team. Some other individuals who are chosen for the team may only be half-heartedly behind the purpose. The leader must create excitement in these members, too.

If you are the leader, begin by letting everyone know you are 100 percent committed to the vision and goals. Show your enthusiasm and willingness to do whatever is necessary to attain the goals. Your enthusiasm may spread to the group. Acknowledge progress the team makes and a job well done.

Let team members know they are valued constituents of the team and you need their opinions and expertise. Tell them they can make a difference for themselves, their coworkers, and the organization.

Exercise: Inspire the Team

If you were the leader of a team, how would you inspire the team members to get behind the vision and do their best work? _____

_____

_____

_____

_____

_____

MANAGE THE TEAM

Appointed leaders manage some teams; other teams have no distinct leader but are managed by all the team members. Chapter 6, "Filling the Leader/Facilitator Role," provides guidelines for those teams managed by leaders or facilitators.

SET THE POLICIES AND PROCEDURES

Once the team is in place, it's necessary to establish policies and procedures. The leader can establish them, or all the team members can contribute. The main thing is to get the policies down in writing. To establish policies and procedures, answer the sampling of questions that follow or compose your own depending on your circumstances.

- ◆ What is the team's purpose?

- ◆ What roles will each person occupy?

- ◆ What duties will each person perform?

- ◆ How will the progress people make toward their individual goals be measured?

- ◆ How often will progress be measured?

- ◆ What will happen if a team member does not make sufficient progress?

- ◆ How often will members be required to attend meetings?

- ◆ What are the consequences of a team member missing team meetings?

- ◆ How will the team arrive at decisions if there is no consensus of opinion?

- ◆ What are the consequences of disruptive behavior?

Exercise: Set Team Policies

The next time you are a member of a team, list the following policies and procedures you feel the team should abide by. _____

_____

_____

_____

_____

_____

_____

Exercise: Determine Consequences

Make a list of the consequences that should be dispensed to team members who do not perform their tasks efficiently and in a timely manner, who are consistently late or miss meetings, and who do not cooperate with other team members.

_____

_____

_____

_____

_____

_____

HOLD TEAM MEMBERS ACCOUNTABLE

Team members must be cognizant of the need to hold themselves and every other team member accountable for attaining the team's goals. Each member will likely have individual tasks to perform as well as the responsibility for attaining the team's goals.

Individual members must perform with a high degree of proficiency when carrying out their responsibilities. No one should sit back and rely on the other team members to do the work. All members must see to it that each person performs at optimum levels. If someone is not contributing, other team members might end up copying the behavior. The team should not permit poor work habits to continue but should take the action detailed in the policies and procedures laid out when the team was established.

Team members can hold themselves accountable by doing the following:

- Performing assigned tasks to the best of their ability
- Meeting deadlines
- Striving to do their best
- Taking initiative
- Admitting mistakes and working to rectify them
- Assessing their progress
- Keeping their word
- Abiding by company policies and procedures
- Maintaining integrity

Not all team members perform up to standards all the time. The team leader or the team members may be required to deal with unproductive members. Therefore, they will want answers to the following questions:

- How will progress be measured?
- How will the team be evaluated to see if goals are being met?
- Who will evaluate the team's work?
- How will members be held accountable for not completing their individual tasks?
- What are the consequences if team members do not perform their tasks at all?
- Who will enforce the consequences if individuals do not perform their tasks satisfactorily?
- What are the consequences if the team does not meet the team goals?

Exercise: Hold Yourself Accountable

When you are called upon to work on a team, make a list of the ways in which you can hold yourself accountable for meeting your individual team goals.

_____

_____

_____

_____

_____

_____

Make a list of ways in which you can hold other team members accountable.

_____

_____

_____

_____

_____

_____

_____

PROVIDE RESOURCES

The right resources are crucial to a team's success. Typical team resources include, but are not limited to, the following:

- ✦ Time
- ✦ Money
- ✦ Supplies
- ✦ Equipment
- ✦ Facilities
- ✦ Information
- ✦ Knowledge
- ✦ Skills
- ✦ Experts
- ✦ Training

Team members are important resources due to their knowledge, skills, and expertise. Training is another important resource that can be used to impart or improve lacking abilities.

Once they are chosen, team members must be given enough time to meet with one another and to work on the team's goals. If deadlines to meet goals are unrealistic, the team will be hard-pressed to succeed.

If money and supplies are required to meet the team's goals, the organization must provide them in sufficient quantities. The team must have an appropriate place to perform their tasks and the right equipment on hand for their use and availability when they need it.

The team should be given the opportunity to determine which resources would be beneficial to them.

Exercise: Determine Team Resources

The next time you are on a team, make a list of resources you feel would be necessary for the team to complete its goals.

_____

_____

_____

_____

_____

_____

_____

Exercise: Choose the Team

Fill in the following blanks the next time you are called on to create a team.

Purpose for the team _____

Team's goals _____

_____

_____

_____

_____

Expertise needed to achieve the team's goals _____

_____

_____

_____

_____

Number of team members required _____

Team leader _____

Individual roles and goals _____

_____

_____

_____

_____

How the team will be monitored _____

_____

_____

_____

_____

Person who will monitor the team _____

Consequences for not completing individual tasks _____

_____

_____

_____

_____

Resources needed _____

_____

_____

_____

Deadline to complete team goals _____

RESTRUCTURE THE TEAM

Team members who continuously work on the same team may lose their effectiveness over time. By attacking goals and problems from the same perspective time and again, team members lose the creative edge to problem-solving and coming up with innovative ideas. Their ability to expand their thinking is limited, thereby restricting their ability to devise original concepts and solutions. Consider integrating new members into the team, or assemble all new team members.

3 Setting Team Roles and Goals

Effective teams have clearly defined roles and goals among the members. A team leader can appoint individuals to specific roles, or the team members can decide their own roles. Likewise, the leader or the members can establish the team's overall goals and the goals and associated tasks of individual members.

Whatever method is used, each person's role must be clearly defined so there is no question as to how that individual fits into the larger picture of achieving the team's goals. Subsequently, clarity is imperative when explaining the team's goals and defining what each team member is expected to accomplish. Any misunderstandings about roles and goals are potential missteps the team cannot afford to take.

DEFINING GOALS

The overall mission dictates the purpose for establishing a team. That mission will also be used to define the team's goals. To achieve success, all team members must understand and support both the team's mission and the goals.

Besides the team goals, individuals will be assigned tasks related to the mission and team goals. These tasks then comprise the members' individual goals. It is essential that every team member understands her goals and how to go about accomplishing them. If someone does not thoroughly understand what she is to do, it will impact the overall team goal and possibly deter the other members from attaining their goals. For example, if a researcher fails to perform, other members may not be able to put together their part of the team project. Individual goals must be coordinated so every team member's goal is consistent with attaining the overall team goals.

When the leader defines the team goals and assigns individual team member goals, she should determine if team members understand what they are to do. The key word is *understand*. The team members may have heard the leader's directives, but that does not mean each individual understands the full meaning intended. In addition to being as clear and specific as possible when defining goals, the leader must establish whether the team understood. Perhaps the leader could have each person restate the directive or be quizzed on his specific duties.

When defining team goals, consider the following questions:

✦   What are the team goals?

✦   Who will determine the team goals?

✦   How should the work be divided among team members?

✦   Who should perform each task related to the goals?

✦   How can the leader be sure each team member understands his individual goals?

✦   How should team members perform their tasks so they will reach their goals?

✦   How will the team ensure each team member's goals are met satisfactorily?

✦   How will the team know when each team member's goals are met?

✦   What will the team do if team members' goals are not achieved?

✦   How will the team know when the overall team goals have been achieved?

✦   What will happen if the team fails to achieve the overall goals?

The next time you are on a team, complete the following checklist.

Understanding Goals	Yes	No
I know the team goals.		
I know and understand what my specific contributions must be to meet the team's goals.		
I have set my personal goals.		
I know the deadline for completing my goals.		

Understanding Goals	Yes	No
I understand how completing my individual goals will assist the team in meeting its goals.		
I am willing to do what is necessary to reach my goals.		
I have created an action plan for attaining my goals, including breaking complex tasks into smaller steps.		
I will manage my time to meet my deadline.		
I will monitor the progress I make toward my goals.		
I will hold myself accountable for attaining my goals.		
I am committed to my goals.		
I am committed to the team goals.		

You should have answered yes to each item in the checklist. Work toward correcting any negative answers.

SETTING TEAM GOALS

Team members work toward achieving a common goal for which the team was created. As mentioned earlier, the team members also have their own individual goals or tasks they must complete as their part in attaining the overall team goals.

All the team goals should be specific, measurable, and realistic. It will be difficult for team members to perform efficiently if they are unclear about why they are working together or what they are supposed to achieve individually and as a team.

The team goals should be relevant to the team's purpose and attainable by its members. Otherwise, people will have a difficult time committing. When team members are shown the benefits of achieving the team's goals, they are more likely to follow through.

Goals must be specific. Instead of saying, "I will do what I am asked to do," say something like, "I will research the latest trend in software sales by March 1, and I will compile my report by March 5." Try to be as specific as possible.

As previously stated, team members will have individual goals to complete that contribute to the team goals. Individual goals must be aligned with the team's goals. These individual goals must be challenging enough to motivate and excite members but also be realistic. Some team members may agree to a goal and later find out they cannot meet the goal because it was not what they thought they agreed to or because they do not have the skills or knowledge to perform the tasks necessary to achieve the goal. Some members may agree because they do not want to say no to their teammates. Those team members who do not believe they can attain a goal will be defeated from the start, as will members who are not enthused about their goals.

When setting your individual goal, be specific and realistic. Know your deadline, what is expected of you, and the skills and resources you need to perform your duties. Develop a way to measure your progress and periodically determine how far you have come and how far you need to go to reach your goal. For example, if your job is to research a particular trend by the end of the month, determine how long it will take to do your research in the time remaining until your deadline. Create a timeline, and check your progress against it. You will also want to judge the quality of your work and how it measures up to the team's standards.

Not only must goals be attained in a timely manner, but the quality of the work associated with the goals must be exemplary. Individuals whose work does not meet the team criteria will bring down the standards of the entire team.

Exercise: Set Team and Individual Goals

Fill in the following blanks the next time you must set goals for a team project.

The team goals are _____

_____

_____

_____

_____

The team goals are important because _____

_____

_____

_____

_____

My individual goals for the team are _____

_____

_____

_____

_____

My goals relate to the overall goals of the team by _____

_____

_____

_____

I need to complete my goals by _____

_____

MAPPING OUT A PLAN

It is difficult to attain goals without having a clear idea of what to do and how to do it. Map out a plan for reaching your goals by asking yourself:

- ✦ What is the best way to go about achieving my goals?
- ✦ What skills and knowledge do I need?
- ✦ Do I have access to adequate resources?
- ✦ Do I need to rely on other team members to help me reach my goals?
- ✦ What is my deadline?
- ✦ How long do I estimate it will take to reach my goals?
- ✦ Am I willing to do whatever is necessary to attain my goals?
- ✦ What step can I take right now toward attaining my goals?
- ✦ How will I know if I am making progress?
- ✦ How will I know when I have attained my goals?
- ✦ How will I hold myself accountable?

Break your goal down into logically arranged, manageable steps you can take. Create your timeline, and assign the criteria for measuring your progress. Put your plan into action. Focus and remain positive. Be flexible about adjusting your plan if you find you are not making sufficient progress. Make necessary changes in the steps you have created.

Exercise: Create an Action Plan

The next time you are on a team, create an action plan for each of the goals you are assigned to complete.

My goals are _____

_____

_____

The date to begin my goals is _____

The steps I need to take to reach my goals are _____

_____

_____

_____

_____

The skills and knowledge I need to complete my goals include _____

_____

_____

_____

_____

My timeline for committing to my goals is _____

_____

_____

I will measure my goals by _____

_____

_____

_____

I will hold myself accountable by _____

_____

_____

_____

I will know I have reached my goals when _____

_____

_____

_____

If I do not attain my goals, it will affect the team in this way _____

_____

_____

_____

If I attain my goals, it will benefit the team in this way _____

_____

_____

_____

FOCUSING ON GOALS

All team members must focus on the team goals and on their individual goals. It can be easy to set goals and say you will achieve them, but it's difficult to follow through. The key is to stay focused on your goals and do what you need to do to achieve them. Create a clear picture in your mind. Think of your goal as a target you must hit by a specific deadline, and focus your time and energy on hitting that target.

Follow the steps you have mapped out for reaching your goals. Prioritize your tasks and manage your time so you will have sufficient time to complete your regular duties and your goals for the team.

Why do some people fail to reach goals? They fail for a number of reasons including, but not limited to, the following:

+ Confused by the goal's description
+ Uncertain about what the team wants them to do
+ Have no idea how to do the task associated with achieving the goal
+ Do not have the ability to do the tasks leading to achieving the goal
+ Do not have sufficient time to work on the goal
+ Have no plan for reaching the goal
+ Do not have sufficient resources to perform the tasks associated with the goal
+ Distracted
+ Unmotivated; lazy
+ Unfocused
+ Dislike performing the tasks assigned
+ Do not believe achieving the goal is possible
+ Are noncommittal

If uncertainty and confusion inhibit you or you are not really sure what to do and how to do it, ask for clarification and assistance from your teammates. Remember, the team is counting on you to perform your tasks. Do what needs to be done to finish your tasks. If you do not have the necessary skills, ask for training or ask if you can switch goals with someone who does have the skills.

You may encounter any number of obstacles while working toward your goals. Develop a strategy to deal with them. Consider the obstacle a chance to enhance your creative problem-solving skills. For instance, if resources you need to do your tasks are not available, seek a way to do without the resources or look for another means of obtaining the resources.

If what you are doing to reach your goals does not work, change tactics. What can you do differently? Could someone else on the team give you some advice? Are there other resources you can take advantage of? Do not get discouraged, but believe you can succeed.

Exercise: Assess Your Goals

Think about a time you set and achieved a goal. What do you feel contributed most to your reaching this goal?

_____

_____

_____

Think about a time you set a goal but did not achieve it. What do you feel contributed most to your failing to reach the goal? _____

_____

_____

_____

Think about a goal you did not achieve. Is there anything you feel you could have done to attain the goal? Explain your answer. _____

_____

_____

Tips for Achieving Goals

- ✦ Make goals specific.
- ✦ Write down your goals.
- ✦ Set a deadline.
- ✦ Create an action plan and a timeline.
- ✦ Strategize and prioritize steps to take toward attaining your goals.
- ✦ Take steps daily toward achieving your goals.
- ✦ Eliminate obstacles to your goals.
- ✦ Ignore distractions.
- ✦ Remain positive.
- ✦ Be persistent; stay focused.
- ✦ Keep the benefits of reaching your goals in mind.
- ✦ Be flexible.
- ✦ Focus your energy and time on your goals.
- ✦ Develop criteria for evaluating your goals.
- ✦ Measure your progress.
- ✦ Change your strategy if it is not working.
- ✦ Hold yourself accountable for taking action toward your goals.

ROLES

Members may be assigned specific roles toward accomplishing the overall team goal, they may have multiple roles, or they may rotate roles within the group. Their roles may depend on where they are needed at a particular time. Roles should be assigned according to what needs to be done and who can best do it.

If team members do not fulfill their roles, they or their roles may have to be eliminated from the team. For instance, a leader who is not doing his job might be removed from the group and replaced with another team member. A member who holds the role of troubleshooter but who cannot or will not solve problems may have to be replaced, or the team's success will be negatively affected.

Types of team roles might include those of leader, researcher, information assembler, expert consultant, manufacturer, trainer, assistant, and the like. A role might not include a title. A team member's role might simply be to do her assigned task and be available to assist other team members.

The leader may be charged with assigning roles, or the team members themselves might decide on the appropriate roles. To be fair and minimize resistance and conflicts, all members should be required to contribute equally to reaching the team's goals.

The team should have a procedure to follow if a team member does not uphold his role. For instance, if a researcher fails to provide the necessary information he has been charged with finding, what are the consequences? If the leader proves to be inadequate, what steps should be taken?

Roles are not necessarily firm; sometimes team members rotate roles. For example, a person may take the lead for assembling the team and assigning tasks and then turn over the leadership to another team member. Someone may be a researcher at the start and end up doing technical work later.

What should you consider when deciding team roles? Consider the following:

- ✦ Knowledge
- ✦ Skills
- ✦ Training
- ✦ Experience; background
- ✦ Values; perspective
- ✦ The nature of the task
- ✦ Motivation; commitment
- ✦ Personal traits

The next time you are on a team, complete the following checklist.

Understanding My Role	Yes	No
I know my role in the team.		
I understand what is expected of me in this role.		
I know and understand how my specific role contributes toward meeting the team's goals.		
I have the knowledge and skills necessary for this role.		

Understanding My Role	Yes	No
I am willing to do what is necessary to satisfy my role's responsibilities.		
I will hold myself accountable for fulfilling the duties of my role on the team.		
I know the roles of others on the team and how they impact me.		

You should have answered yes to each item in the checklist. Work toward correcting any negative answers.

Exercise: Assess Team Roles

The next time you work on a team, think about the roles assigned to team members and decide if you agree with the roles or if you would change them in any way.

Who decided the team roles? _____

Would you change any of the roles? If so, what changes would you make? _____

_____

_____

_____

Would you add additional roles? If so, what roles would you add? _____

_____

_____

_____

Do you feel team members fulfilled their assigned roles satisfactorily? _____

_____

_____

_____

_____

4 Considering Culture, Competition, Cooperation, and Communication

Team members rely on the cooperation and collaboration of others within the team and possibly outside the team to accomplish the team's goal. Obviously, team members must get along to reach their goals.

Team members must show support and respect for one another. They must hold themselves and others accountable; otherwise, the team will be disorderly and fragmented. The result will make reaching the team's goal difficult if not impossible.

CULTURE

The team's culture is composed of the informal, unwritten rules and practices by which the team members function. This culture pertains to the team members' interactions, attitudes, traditions, views, work ethic, knowledge, skills, and so forth. Although every company has its unique culture, the teams formed within the company may also have their own cultures. For instance, company employees may have a particular way of doing a task, but a team formed by some of those employees may come up with a different way of confronting the same task. The team fashions its own culture as the team's norms are established.

Personal traits of team members affect the culture of the group. A culture that includes a strong work ethic, highly skilled and knowledgeable experts, tolerance, commitment, respect among team members, accountability, and a pleasant atmosphere that encourages cooperation is conducive to success. Members who are positive, focused, energetic, cooperative, capable, and willing bring much to the team. A team lacking in these traits has a difficult time succeeding.

Demographics may affect team behavior. Successful teams are composed of members who have common interests and whose personalities are suited to one another. For example, young members' perspectives may differ greatly from older ones; women may take a different view from men, and so forth. These differences can make for a balanced team and well-rounded team members if all members adapt and commit to understanding each other.

Diversity among team members is likely to increase views and perspectives, which can lead to more ideas and greater creativity. Therefore, team members must respect one another's viewpoints and reach accord to benefit from this diversity. This personal growth is one of the many benefits of teamwork.

Team members who hope to fit in should act in an acceptable manner according to the team's culture. If members have a difficult time figuring out the team's culture, they may inadvertently do something to cause problems with their teammates or even sabotage the team's goals. The best way to determine the team's culture is to observe how others on the team behave. Learning the answers to the questions that follow will help significantly.

Team culture issues may include, but are not limited to, the answers to the following questions:

- ✦ Who does what task?
- ✦ Who assigns the tasks?
- ✦ Who determines the quality of performance?
- ✦ Who is the team leader?
- ✦ How does the leader relate to others?
- ✦ How should the tasks be completed?
- ✦ Who holds what role on the team?
- ✦ How do team members relate to one another?
- ✦ How do team members perceive others' abilities and performance?
- ✦ What attitudes are prevalent on the team?
- ✦ In what way is the team diversified?
- ✦ Who will offer advice and assistance when asked?
- ✦ Is anyone overbearing and off-putting?
- ✦ Who completes tasks on time and who does not?
- ✦ Who keeps confidences and who does not?
- ✦ Which members are the most respected on the team?
- ✦ What skills and knowledge do team members possess?
- ✦ Who are the team experts?
- ✦ How do team members arrive at team decisions?

+ What communication procedures are in place?
+ Is there a team leader?
+ Does the leader have an open-door policy?
+ What are the consequences of not performing assigned tasks?

Besides bringing a unique perspective to the team, members with diverse views could become the source of conflict. Chapter 9, "Handling Conflict," provides tips for conflict resolution among team members.

If the team culture becomes a deterrent to reaching goals, the leader or the members may have to take steps to change the culture by restructuring the way the members interact or by restructuring the team by changing members.

Exercise: Determine Team Culture

The next time you are a member of a team, see if you can determine the team's culture.

What are the informal team rules?

_____

_____

_____

_____

Do you feel the diversity of the team members is beneficial to the team? If the team is not diverse, do you feel it should be? Explain your answers.

_____

_____

_____

_____

Describe various team members' attitudes.

_____

_____

_____

Describe how the team members interact.

_____

_____

_____

Describe how the team leaders interact with other members.

_____

_____

_____

_____

Do you feel the team culture is conducive to attaining team goals? Explain your answer.

_____

_____

_____

_____

Do you feel anything should change within the team regarding its culture? Explain your answer.

_____

_____

_____

_____

COMPETITION

Healthy competition can be positive. A friendly challenge among team members can spark excitement, increasing team member enthusiasm while they complete tasks and work through problems, making the process of attaining goals a pleasant experience. However, if the competition between team members sparks jealousy and backstabbing, everyone stands to lose. Team members will become disgruntled and discouraged quickly.

Team leaders should monitor their team members' behavior to keep informed of rising tensions or conflicts associated with competition. Unhealthy competition should be suppressed immediately.

In addition to team members competing with one another, various teams within an organization might compete with one another. Again, such competition should be a source of pride and camaraderie, not contention.

Exercise: Assess Team Competition

Think about a team on which you have worked. Were the team members competitive? If so, in what way?

_____

_____

_____

Do you feel friendly competition among team members is constructive? Explain your answer.

_____

_____

_____

_____

_____

COOPERATION

In addition to being chosen for their skills and their ability to contribute to the overall team goals, members should be chosen for their compatibility. Team members will undoubtedly express different points of view in their dealings with each other, but compatible individuals will find a way to work together. The objective should be to reach an agreement that benefits the team and its goals, not the individual members. To that end, each team member must be willing to cooperate and be open to compromise.

Cooperative team members also pull their own weight, commit to the team goals, obey procedures, respect one another, and follow through with their tasks. They avoid power plays and team politics that deadlock the team. They coordinate their goals and tasks with those of the other team members.

Team members who do not cooperate with one another disrupt team harmony and impair the team's success. Complainers, slackers, saboteurs, and the like destroy teams. Chapter 9 provides tips for handling problem team members.

Team politics can disrupt team accord. For instance, if team members feel the leader is biased or is showing favoritism, they will be understandably upset. To the extent possible, keep power plays, cliques, backstabbing, gossiping, lying, taking credit for another's work, favoritism, and the like out of the team. Follow the established team procedures for admonishing disruptive team members.

Ask these questions to determine the level of cooperation among team members:

✦ Does the team leader encourage cooperation among members?

✦ Are team members willing to collaborate with one other to meet goals?

✦ Are team members willing to cooperate with outside resources (other departments, customers)?

✦ What are the consequences if team members refuse to cooperate?

✦ How can you get uncooperative team members to cooperate?

✦ Does the team have open communication?

✦ Do team members trust one another?

✦ Do team members support one another?

✦ Are team members unbiased and accepting of one another?

✦ Do team members display appropriate, positive behavior?

✦ Do team members perform their assigned tasks effectively?

✦ Do team members follow the team's procedures and policies?

The ability to negotiate is a key skill for team members and leaders. They must find constructive ways to deal with differing values, ideas, and suggestions. Negotiation is a way to reach some kind of agreement that satisfies all team members. Chapter 7, "Making Group Decisions and Negotiating," offers more information on negotiation.

Assess your cooperative character traits by completing the following checklist.

Cooperative Character Traits Checklist	Exhibit	Hope to Improve	Do Not Exhibit
Pleasant			
Positive			
Realistic			
Honest			
Practical			
Adaptable			
Reasonable			
Patient			
Kind			
Committed			
Empathetic			
Tolerant			
Supportive			
Tactful			
Respectful			
Accommodating			

You should have indicated that you exhibit these personal traits. Work toward correcting any traits you do not possess or that you hope to improve.

Having problem solvers on the team is advantageous in managing disagreements and discussions. Team members must be able to work together for the good of the team, which includes building cohesiveness within the team.

COMMUNICATION

The lines of communication should be kept open at all times with everyone involved. Team leaders should maintain an open-door policy with team members. Each individual on the team should communicate effectively with every other member, including the leader.

Everyone on the team needs to follow directions and share information. Any confusing information should be clarified as soon as possible. The person giving directives should be clear, and the person receiving them should speak up if she does not understand.

Team members should be kept informed. When several people on the team are sharing information, confusion can result if the information is not conveyed in an orderly fashion. Members should take turns presenting the information and should be reasonably sure the others understand it before moving on to the next team member's presentation.

Team members should be encouraged to speak up and ask for help if they get in over their heads or do not understand what they are doing.

Speaking

Sharing worthwhile information is critical to teams. Those charged with distributing information must do so accurately and clearly.

When you are sharing information, speak loud enough to be heard and at a moderate pace. Present ideas in a logical order, and be specific. Use easy-to-understand language, avoiding slang and jargon that may be unfamiliar to team members. Try to relate your information to what team members already know. Break down complex information into manageable bits, and ask teammates if they understand. If they do not, start over. Repeat the information or try another approach to disseminating it. Have another teammate who understands what you said explain it to the other team members. Use appropriate visual aids when necessary. Finally, eliminate as many distractions as possible.

Listening

Listening is another critical skill for team members. Many times people hear what is said, but they are not listening, which involves processing what they heard. Team members cannot gain knowledge or gather essential facts if they do not pay attention during information sharing.

When you are listening to a teammate, concentrate on what she is saying. Relate what you already know to the new information. Write down pertinent information, especially if you will need it later. Avoid jumping to conclusions or finishing the teammate's sentences. If you are confused by anything your teammate said, ask for clarification. Clear up any misunderstandings at once.

Communicating Nonverbally

Team members often communicate without saying anything by using nonverbal communication. A team member's silence, texting, napping, shaking the head, nodding the head in agreement, smiling, frowning, turning away from the speaker, leaning toward the speaker, crossing arms, tapping feet or drumming fingers, and so forth are all ways an individual communicates his feelings without saying a word.

Speaking Tips

- ◆ Plan what you are going to say.

- ◆ Arrange ideas logically.

- ◆ Use easy-to-understand language.

- ◆ Speak clearly and loudly enough to be heard.

- ◆ Be specific.

- ◆ Use proper grammar and pronunciation.

- ◆ Repeat key information.

- ◆ Vary your inflection.

- ◆ Clarify confusing points.

- ◆ Gauge your listeners to determine if they are paying attention.

- ◆ Eliminate distractions if possible (talking over you, noise, poor lighting, and so on).

- ◆ Use appropriate visuals if helpful.

- ◆ Be mindful of your nonverbal communication.

- ◆ Ask listeners if they understand.

Listening Tips

- ◆ Pay attention; stay mentally engaged.

- ◆ Analyze what is said.

- ◆ Relate what is said to what you already know about the subject.

- ◆ Avoid jumping to conclusions.

- ◆ Ask for clarification if you need it.

- ◆ Avoid preconceived notions.

- ◆ Take notes if necessary.

- ◆ Restate the speaker's words in your mind.

- ◆ Avoid tuning out the speaker.

- ◆ Avoid using negative nonverbal communication.

- ◆ Do not let the speaker's negative habits distract you.

- ◆ Minimize distractions.

Nonverbal Communication Tips

✦   Smile.

✦   Nod in agreement.

✦   Look at the other person while speaking or listening.

✦   Keep an open stance.

✦   Avoid tapping feet or drumming fingers.

✦   Avoid clicking pens or tapping pencils.

Complete the following checklist.

Checklist for Effective Communication	Yes	No
I share my knowledge and skills.		
I speak clearly and use easy-to-understand language.		
I vary my tone and maintain a normal volume.		
I present ideas logically in easy-to-understand language.		
I use proper grammar.		
I use appropriate visual aids when necessary.		
I listen carefully to other team members.		
I ask for clarification if I do not understand something a teammate says.		
I learn from my teammates.		
I relate what I know to what is said.		
I avoid jumping to conclusions.		
I take notes when necessary.		
I use positive nonverbal communication.		
I do not let the speaker's negative habits distract me.		

You should have answered yes to each item in the checklist. Work toward correcting any negative answers.

Exercise: Assess Team Communication Procedures

Think about a team on which you have worked. Did the team have a communication procedure in place? If yes, what was the procedure? _____

_____

_____

_____

_____

Do you feel team members communicated efficiently with one another? Why or why not?

_____

_____

_____

_____

How do you feel communication among team members can be improved?

_____

_____

_____

_____

5 Motivating Team Members

Entire books have been written about ways to motivate yourself and others. You may want to consult some of these books if you feel you have a serious problem motivating yourself or you need to motivate your teammates.

Although it can be difficult to motivate certain people, some individuals are motivated by external rewards such as money, extra time off, and accolades, whereas others are self-motivated and perform regardless of the rewards. This chapter presents some tips for motivating the team as a whole and as individual team members.

MOTIVATION

Motivated individuals perform at a higher level than their counterparts. They push themselves to get the job done even when they do not feel like it. Therefore, motivating team members will have a positive effect on team achievement. Teams composed of motivated individuals are always moving toward the completion of team goals.

Team Motivation

Motivated team members get things done. They have positive character traits, expect success, remain upbeat despite obstacles and setbacks, complete tasks in a timely manner, and persist. Motivated team members have high expectations of themselves and their teammates. They are open to new experiences and learn from their mistakes.

How can you motivate team members when you are their leader? Getting team members to see the value in what they are doing and to expect to succeed as a group may encourage them to become self-motivated. Declare the importance of the tasks assigned to the team members. Let them know they were specifically chosen for the tasks based on their expertise and skills. Enthusiastically state the high expectations you have for the team, and challenge them to meet your expectations. Be their cheerleader, and let them know you will support them every step of the way. Give examples of people who have succeeded in similar cases.

Sometimes team members are overwhelmed by the nature and size of their tasks. Be aware of their struggles, and suggest to them that they break down tasks into manageable parts. Offer your assistance; be a mentor.

If you are in a position to provide extrinsic rewards, such as money, time off, awards, and the like, to team members who reach their goals, tell them. Otherwise, concentrate on boosting their internal rewards like the ability to succeed, value to the company and teammates, and pride in a job well done.

Give team members a reason to be motivated. Create a worthwhile vision for the team and explain the benefits of supporting it. Show them you are 100 percent committed to the team vision and goals.

Here are some factors that might weaken the team's motivation:

- ✦ Team members who do not do their assigned tasks
- ✦ Conflict among members
- ✦ No information sharing among members
- ✦ Team members being treated unfairly by the leader
- ✦ Incompetent leadership
- ✦ Team members showing up unprepared for meetings
- ✦ No knowledge and skill sharing among members
- ✦ Low self-confidence among one or more members
- ✦ Unclear vision and goals for the team
- ✦ Continuous failures
- ✦ Not enough meetings to discuss and work on team goals
- ✦ Negative personality traits of one or more members
- ✦ Too many ineffective team members
- ✦ No direction or guidance
- ✦ Lack of necessary skills and knowledge
- ✦ Lack of necessary resources
- ✦ Lack of cooperation among members
- ✦ Intimidation tactics used by the leader

As the leader, you can help team members find the motivation they need to attain the team's goals. Begin by creating a clear vision of what the team must accomplish. Set goals or have the team set goals for realizing the vision. Make it clear to everyone involved how important the vision is for the entire organization. Emphasize how essential each team member is in attaining the team goals. As individual tasks are assigned, be sure the members charged with completing the tasks know why they must succeed.

Monitor the team's progress, and have clearly defined consequences in place. If a member is unprepared for meetings or does not complete tasks in a timely manner, hold her accountable. Show no favoritism.

Provide the resources needed to complete the tasks: people, data, technical and other equipment, supplies, time, place, and anything else team members require in their pursuits. Without access to proper resources, the team will have a difficult or impossible time completing their tasks. If team members need more training and education to complete their goals, arrange for seminars, courses, and mentors.

Specify a place for the team to meet and discuss goals and tasks, and make it convenient for all members to attend. Allow sufficient time for members to meet and for them to complete their tasks. Encourage members to routinely share their knowledge, skills, and progress on their individual tasks and goals. Keep the lines of communication open between members and the leader. If discussions get out of hand or conflicts arise, settle them quickly and fairly.

Encourage team members to motivate one another. If a team member slacks off, it could have a negative impact on other members who may decide to copy the poor behavior. When members show up ill-prepared for meetings and miss deadlines, everyone is affected.

Tips Leaders Can Use to Motivate Team Members

- ✦ Clearly state the team's vision and goals and their importance to the organization.
- ✦ Assign goals to the individual team members, and stress the importance of attaining them.
- ✦ Keep everyone informed about progress on goals.
- ✦ Have consequences in place for not completing tasks or for doing poor-quality work.
- ✦ Encourage open communication.
- ✦ Stress the importance of being ready for meetings and completing assigned tasks.
- ✦ Observe team members regularly.
- ✦ Be fair to everyone on the team; do not show favoritism.
- ✦ Find ways to motivate individuals who need it.
- ✦ Provide necessary resources, including people, time, training, equipment, supplies, and the like.
- ✦ Deal with complainers and conflict.
- ✦ Encourage team members to support one another.

Individual Motivation

Self-motivation entails compelling yourself to do your tasks even when you do not feel like doing them. By consistently pushing yourself and holding yourself accountable for following through on tasks, you increase the chances that self-motivation will become a habit.

Sometimes thinking about what you have to do is more difficult than actually doing it. Do not procrastinate; push yourself to take action one step at a time. Keep going until you complete your assigned tasks or reach your goals. Be diligent and persistent, and do not let obstacles hold you back. Get help from other team members if you need it.

Hold the team's vision in your mind, and remind yourself of your importance to the team. Believe you are a valuable asset and that only you can do your specifically assigned tasks.

Tips for Motivating Yourself

- ✦ Keep yourself in a positive state.
- ✦ Downplay problems.
- ✦ Stay informed.
- ✦ Monitor your progress.
- ✦ Surround yourself with supportive people.
- ✦ Model people who have succeeded in attaining similar goals.
- ✦ Persist.
- ✦ Keep moving toward your goals.
- ✦ Use a to-do list.
- ✦ Keep the end goal in mind.
- ✦ Create and use daily affirmations.
- ✦ Conceive a clear vision of your goals.
- ✦ Know the importance of reaching your goals.

Complete the following checklist.

Motivating Self and Team Members	Yes	No
I have a clear vision of the team's goals and my individual goals.		
I realize the value in completing my tasks.		
I expect success.		
I do not let setbacks and obstacles derail my efforts.		
I maintain a positive attitude.		
I complete tasks in a timely manner.		
I monitor my progress.		
I have high expectations of myself.		
I have high expectations of my team members.		

Motivating Self and Team Members	Yes	No
I produce quality work at all times and encourage teammates to do the same.		
I hold myself and my teammates accountable for completing tasks and attaining goals.		
I am open to new ideas and experiences.		
I learn from my mistakes.		
I push myself to complete my tasks.		
I do not procrastinate when I have a job to do.		
I support my teammates.		

You should have answered yes to each item in the checklist. Work toward correcting any negative answers.

Exercise: Assess Team Member Motivation

The next time you are on a team, observe how other team members seem to motivate themselves to complete tasks. Can you emulate them? Write your observations here.

_____

_____

_____

_____

_____

Exercise: Motivate Yourself

Create a list of ways you can motivate yourself to accomplish your goals. Include behaviors that worked for you in the past.

_____

_____

_____

_____

_____

_____

Exercise: Assess Your Behavior

Think about a time you were part of a team and had tasks to complete but put them off because you were unmotivated. Answer the following questions.

What should I have done that I did not do? _____

_____

_____

Why did I procrastinate? _____

_____

_____

_____

How did my procrastination affect the other team members? _____

_____

_____

_____

How did my procrastination affect my team's attaining its goals?_____

_____

_____

_____

What can I do in the future to avoid procrastinating? _____

_____

_____

_____

VISUALIZE

Create a vision in the minds of team members of what success will look like whenever the team has reached its goals. Try to construct a vision that will motivate them by getting members excited about the challenge of reaching the goals. Stress the opportunity they have been given to make a valued contribution to the organization. Give them the big picture of where their contributions fit in and how they will impact the organization. Let them know the tasks assigned to them may not be ideal, but they are all part of that big picture and vital to the team's goals.

When you are assigned individual team goals, create a clear vision for each goal. Picture yourself successfully performing the required tasks to achieve the goals. Keep the vision of a positive outcome firmly in your mind by seeing yourself take the necessary steps toward your goal and picturing the successful outcome. Believe you will achieve your goals.

- ✦ Explain to the team what successfully reaching their goals will look like.
- ✦ Have team members visualize successfully attaining their goals.
- ✦ Tell team members what reaching their goals will mean to the team.
- ✦ Tell the team how failing to attain their goals will hurt the team.
- ✦ Advise the team how reaching their goals will affect the organization.
- ✦ Advise the team how failing to attain their goals will affect the organization.

Exercise: Create Excitement

The next time you are a team leader, create and convey a picture of the team's vision that will excite the team members.

Exercise: Achieve Goals

The next time you are a member of a team, visualize achieving your individual goals and determine how they complete the team's goals. Keep in mind the importance of your goals and the team's goals to the organization as a whole as you picture yourself achieving them.

COMMITMENT

Committed individuals dedicate themselves to their goals and the goals of their teams. They strive to reach goals by devising a plan of action and following through on the tasks that lead to the completion of the goals. Committed team members do their part to ensure all team goals are met in a timely manner.

Team Commitment

All team members must be committed to the team to ensure all tasks are carried out and the goals are met. One person can have a disastrous effect on the team's outcome. For example, if a team member who has been assigned to research information for a report fails to complete his task on time, the other team members who need the information will not be able to complete their goals either. Define for every person the time commitment and level of work required for the team to succeed.

The level of the team's commitment determines its success at arriving at goals. Committed team members do whatever is necessary to reach their goals and the team's goals. They keep pushing toward their goals even if the steps to reach them are tedious or difficult. They consistently turn in quality work.

Noncommittal individuals give up easily. If these individuals are not motivated to complete their tasks, other team members may decide they cannot or will not go it alone; they may lose motivation as well. The leader and the other team members should attempt to motivate the noncommittal team member. If they cannot, it may be necessary to remove that individual from the team.

The team leader must appeal to the team members' sense of pride and professionalism. Ask, "Do you want to be the person who lets the team down?" Make clear the consequences of the team's failure to attain its goals and the consequences for any individuals who are not motivated to complete their tasks. Celebrate the team's successes.

Individual Commitment

As an individual team member, you have a responsibility to uphold your end of the agreement to meet the team's goals and to carry out its vision. Do whatever it takes to reach your goals. Make up your mind that you will treat obstacles as challenges and find solutions. Deal with setbacks and move on.

Find successful people who have attained what you hope to attain, and model them. What did they do to succeed? Can you do the same thing?

Create a to-do list and use it to take daily action toward your goals. Prioritize tasks and focus on the most important step first. Take the next steps and work your way through the list. Congratulate yourself on completing tasks.

Be honest about your progress. When you are stuck, go to the team and ask for help. Another person's thoughts might be just what you need. Brainstorm ideas with the team. Re-create your goals or the steps to attain them.

Complete the following checklist.

Committing to the Team	Yes	No
I have accepted my assigned goals and the tasks.		
I follow through on my commitments.		
I do whatever is necessary to help the team.		
I treat obstacles as challenges to be resolved.		
I monitor my progress and hold myself accountable.		
I am prepared for all team meetings and encourage my teammates to be prepared.		
I seek help from my teammates if I need it.		
I help my teammates when they need it.		
I produce quality work at all times and encourage teammates to do the same.		
I hold myself and my teammates accountable for completing tasks and attaining goals.		
I know the consequences of failing to attain my goals and the team's goals.		

You should have answered yes to each item in the checklist. Work toward correcting any negative answers.

Exercise: Commit to Goals

The next time you are on a team, fill in the following blanks with your plan for committing to your individual goals that support the team's overall goal.

_____

_____

_____

_____

_____

_____

AFFIRMATIONS

Affirmations are positive statements that describe what you want or hope to achieve. They can be used to program thoughts to improve your attitude and outlook. Affirmations can help keep individuals on task, increase their motivation, and attain their goals. The right affirmations can help team members remain positive when their plans go awry. Encourage team members to create affirmations regarding the team's goals. They might say, "I focus my attention on my team's goals," or "I support my team vision."

Individual team members should create affirmations regarding their particular goals and associated tasks. Personal affirmations are composed of declarations the individual desires to achieve. For example, "I take steps every day that bring me closer to my goal."

What you focus on expands; therefore, use positive language when creating affirmations. You do not want negativity to take over because your affirmation declares what you do not want, such as, "I will not fail to attain my goal." A better affirmation would be "I will attain my goal."

Be specific in stating what you hope to accomplish. Use present tense verbs as if you already have whatever you are affirming. Make statements brief and repeat them often so they become embedded in your thoughts.

Exercise: Affirm Your Goals

Think of a personal goal you would like to attain. Create positive affirmations that will help you stay on task and steadily work toward attaining the goal. Write two or three affirmations you feel will help you reach your personal goal.

_____

_____

_____

_____

Exercise: Affirm the Team's Goals

The next time you are on a team, create positive affirmations that will help you stay on task and steadily work toward attaining your goals. When the time comes, write two or three affirmations in the space that follows.

_____

_____

_____

_____

_____

CHALLENGES

When you feel things need to change in regard to the team's progress toward reaching its goals, question the team members' performance. Are they doing everything possible to reach goals? Are they taking necessary risks? Are they focusing their energy and ingenuity on their goals? Are they attacking obstacles with enthusiasm? Are they supporting one another? Do they share information and their expertise with one another?

Sometimes team members are entrenched in familiar patterns to the extent they cannot think their way past obstacles. Encourage team members to move out of their comfort zones and try something different. Have them share how they set and attain goals and encourage them to try some of the techniques other team members use. Brainstorming is a meaningful exercise for coming up with new ideas.

Challenge team members to take risks. Just be sure the risks are appropriate, worth taking, and apt to be valuable. Successful team members set challenging goals and brainstorm ways to attain them. Remind the team of the value of flexible thinking and creativity. If what they are doing to reach goals is not working, perhaps a change of strategy is necessary. Oftentimes what worked in the past is no longer effective.

Encourage team members to ask for help when they need it and to support one another throughout the team's mission. It is far better to ask for help than to fail.

Some situations cannot be controlled. Take control where you can, and adapt to or find a way around issues you cannot control.

6 Filling the Leader/Facilitator Role

The team leader/facilitator role is one of organizer, mediator, supporter, implementer, and doer. The leader conveys the team's vision, establishes the direction to take, and helps team members focus on their roles and tasks.

Team leadership can take different approaches, depending on what the company and the team organizers want to achieve. A successful team needs some type of leadership to spearhead the team members' efforts, keep them on track, and prevent them from falling into disarray through conflict or lack of direction.

DEFINING LEADERS

A leader may be appointed by the company requesting the formation of the team. If so, this leader must be an individual who can relate positively to the team. Another option is that a leader may be chosen by the team members rather than appointed from outside the team. Or the team members may decide not to designate a leader at all, instead opting to have all individual team members participate in facilitating the team's roles, goals, information sharing, decisions, resources, progress, and the like.

One of your duties as a leader is to get your team to understand and contribute to the vision and goals of the team. Let team members know how the team will contribute to the organization's overall vision. Commit to helping team members succeed in supporting the vision and completing their tasks. What can you do to help individual team members? Stress the importance of being a productive member of the team. Encourage them, and show you appreciate them. Model the type of behavior you want them to exhibit.

The leader role often rotates through the team depending on the expertise of the members. If a particular skill or knowledge is needed, the member with that skill or knowledge may become the temporary leader until a different area of expertise is needed. Then the member with that expertise would take over the leadership.

Regardless of the team leadership, the team members must be given the authority to make decisions and to accomplish their goals. If the team cannot implement its ideas and solutions, it cannot succeed.

Exercise: Define Your Leadership Style

Describe your leadership style.

_____

_____

_____

_____

_____

ASSESSING LEADERSHIP SKILLS

A leader's ability to utilize team members' expertise and talents has an enormous bearing on the team's success. Team leaders who know their teammates' strengths and weaknesses are able to better assign roles and tasks to take advantage of their expertise and strengths. They are not afraid to change direction when something or someone is not working.

Leaders must be able to relate to team members in a manner that the members will have confidence in them. Good interpersonal skills are essential if a leader hopes to gain the team members' trust and cooperation. The leader must develop a positive relationship with the team members if she hopes to influence them in a manner beneficial to the team and its goals. Leaders who get to know their team members can take advantage of their strengths and make them feel good about themselves when they succeed and thus create positive morale.

To increase your effectiveness as a leader, observe the strengths and weaknesses of your team members and use that information to the individual's and the team's advantage. Get to know them personally and find things in common so you can build stronger relationships. Show them respect, and let them know they can trust you. Remember that personal encouragement from the leader goes a long way.

You may not always enjoy the people you work with, but as the leader, it is your job to keep the team running at an optimum level. Therefore, find a way to get along with all team members and appreciate what they bring to the team.

Be visible by making yourself accessible to team members. Be proactive in monitoring their progress. Some individuals may not want to admit they need help or have failed to perform their tasks satisfactorily. They may not admit they do not know what to do. Work with them and encourage them to come to you with concerns.

Effective leaders must be good listeners and communicators, as discussed in Chapter 4, "Considering Culture, Competition, Cooperation, and Communication." It is the leader's job to keep the team informed of progress and changes. When team members are left to guess what is happening, they begin to formulate their own opinions, which can lead to inaccurate gossip. Leaders of culturally diverse teams face the additional challenge of interpreting cultural perceptions, viewpoints, and signals, all of which the leaders must address.

Team members who see the leader taking charge, solving problems, and producing results are encouraged to follow her. Poor leaders have a difficult time rousing team members to do their best work.

Strong leaders must have excellent interpersonal and communication skills, including but not limited to the following:

- ✦ A keen understanding of team members
- ✦ The ability to disseminate information and explain clearly
- ✦ The ability to listen without judgment
- ✦ A clear understanding of the team's mission
- ✦ Deep commitment and the ability to influence the other team members to commit
- ✦ Imagination and vision
- ✦ A willingness to make difficult decisions
- ✦ The ability to motivate others
- ✦ Conflict-resolution and problem-solving ability
- ✦ Creativity
- ✦ Expertise
- ✦ Focus and persistence
- ✦ Calm presence; patience
- ✦ Attentiveness to people
- ✦ Flexibility

Would you be an effective team leader? Complete the following checklist.

Team Leader Criteria	Yes	No
I know how to communicate with others in a constructive manner.		
I am a good judge of character.		
I am decisive.		
I have the ability to motivate people.		

Team Leader Criteria	Yes	No
I am a good listener.		
I remain calm under pressure.		
I am willing to make difficult decisions to reach the team's goals.		
I enjoy a challenge.		
I support the team.		
I am willing to discipline teammates if necessary.		
I can adjust to change without complaint.		
I am proactive providing feedback to team members.		
I celebrate my teammates' success.		
I know how to best utilize my teammates' expertise and skills.		
I will uphold the team's and organization's standards for performance.		

You should have answered yes to each item in the checklist. Work toward correcting any negative answers.

Exercise: Assess Interpersonal Skills

Describe your personal traits that will help you be an effective leader.

_____

_____

_____

_____

Describe your personal traits that will detract from your being an effective leader.

_____

_____

_____

_____

MONITORING THE TEAM

How will the team and those who organized it know when the goals are met? Someone must be responsible for monitoring the team's progress or lack thereof. In addition, this person should be able to determine if the team's goals have been met successfully.

Team members should be held to company standards, and they should produce quality results in a timely manner. The team will suffer if individual team members are allowed to turn in substandard work or miss deadlines.

Either the leader or the team members may set the criteria to be used in evaluating goals. This should be done at the first team meeting so everyone has a clear idea of what is expected.

Questions the leader or facilitator may want answers to include these:

✦ What are the team's expectations for meeting the team goals?

✦ What is the leader's expectation for meeting the team's goals?

✦ What criteria will be used in evaluating goals?

✦ What will happen if the team members' expectations are different from the leader's expectations?

✦ Who will monitor the progress of the goals?

✦ Who will monitor the quality of the work?

✦ Who will decide when the goals are met?

✦ How will the team know when the goals are met?

✦ What steps will be taken if progress is not made on goals?

✦ What will happen if goals are not met?

Complete the following checklist.

Monitoring Goals	Yes	No
The team and I know the criteria to be used in monitoring goals and the standard of performance required to meet those goals.		
I know what criteria I will use to monitor the team's goals.		
I know how often I will monitor the team's goals.		
I know what team members should do to meet team goals.		
I know what steps to take if progress is not made on goals.		
I know what to look for to determine if team goals are met.		
I know the consequences of not meeting goals.		
I do not let obstacles stand in the way of reaching my goals or the team's goals.		

You should have answered yes to each item in the checklist. Work toward correcting any negative answers.

Exercise: Monitor the Team

The next time you are a member of a team, analyze how the team is monitored.

Who will monitor the team's progress? _____

_____

_____

What criteria will be used to monitor the team's progress? _____

_____

_____

_____

What are the consequences if team members do not perform satisfactorily?

_____

_____

_____

_____

INCREASING PRODUCTIVITY

Productive team members feel good about themselves and the team. Leaders can help increase productivity by dividing tasks among team members according to their skills and expertise so their efforts yield the best results. Help team members realize their potential. Show them how to organize and prioritize their tasks. They must make sure each person understands what he is to do to produce the results necessary to drive the team forward.

Tell team members how their specific expertise and skills will contribute to the team's vision and goals. Ask them what they need from you, and provide it if possible. Stress to the team the value of working together and how they can accomplish more with their combined talents. Help team members see the need to forgo their individual egos and work together to benefit the team and all its members.

Productive leaders are good role models; show team members how they should perform by producing results yourself. When team members see their leaders actively participating in the tasks necessary to reach goals and making progress toward the attainment of those goals, the members are apt to follow suit. The team's morale and confidence rise and, hopefully, so will productivity.

Effective leaders take an active role in assisting the team. They do not sit back and watch the team perform but instead take action by using their skills and expertise to do their share of the work or to guide team members. They are good at what they do. Leaders are part of the team and must produce along with the other team members. Active leaders get noticed. Establish your credibility as an active member of the team. People respond favorably to leaders who do their part to generate team success.

Let unproductive team members know their actions will not be tolerated. State the consequences for not performing to standards, including the effect on the team's goals and vision.

Exercise: Be an Asset

The next time you are a team leader, create a plan for helping team members be more productive. List ways you will be an asset to the team.

_____

_____

_____

_____

_____

If you are not a leader but the member of team, create a plan for being an asset to the team.

_____

_____

_____

_____

_____

PROVIDING FEEDBACK

Take the time to provide feedback so team members know if they are doing what was asked of them and performing up to standards. Most team members want to know if they are doing their tasks accurately or if they need to change what they are doing to succeed. No one sets out to fail.

Choose your words carefully to show people you care about them and respect them, but let them know you will hold them accountable for completing their tasks. Constructive feedback is crucial to the team's understanding of the quality of their performance. Many times a team member feels she is doing a good job when the leader realizes the work is not up to the organization's standards. The leader then must tactfully tell the team member she is underperforming and tell or show her how to correct the situation.

Treat everyone on the team in a fair and consistent manner. Any show of favoritism among team members will cause conflicts. Hold everyone accountable for performing to the team's and organization's standards.

Competent leaders acknowledge the accomplishments of team members and celebrate their successes. These leaders applaud individual achievements and the team's achievements. Give credit where it is due. As team members gain confidence, their performance may improve.

Feedback is not always positive. Sometimes a leader must discipline team members who do not perform their tasks or who do poor-quality work. Some team members may take offense to the leader's criticism no matter how constructive it is. In such cases, the team's goals and productivity are the priority. If the team member does not improve his performance, he should face the consequences of the team's disciplinary procedures.

Most individuals do not like to confront people, but leaders may have to step up to the task to get things done. When giving negative feedback, always do so in private and in a way that improves the person, not intimidates or embarrasses him. Rather than just say what is wrong, show team members what they should do and how to do it. Make your expectations clear. Help them improve their performance.

MAKING DECISIONS

Sound decision-making skills help the leader guide team members toward solutions. Leaders often have to attend to the most difficult tasks and problems facing the team. Be a problem-solver. Look at the issue from all sides, write down possible solutions, and choose the best solution in your estimation. If that does not work, try something else.

The leader must be sure to consider all information and team opinions to gain a well-rounded view of the situation. The leader should not make all the decisions for the team but rather should encourage all team members to take part in the decision-making process. This ensures the team, not the leader, is in control of its goals.

Sometimes these decisions involve handling personnel matters, which can be awkward when the leader does not want to alienate team members. However, if the team is to operate smoothly, the leader must take control and do whatever is necessary to advance the team.

Making decisions means taking risks. Not all of the leader's decisions will be right or popular, but she must learn to weigh the options and make the best decision possible in any given situation.

Leaders should also be willing to admit when they make a mistake and then try to correct it. Chapter 7, "Making Group Decisions and Negotiating," offers additional tips for making decisions.

SHARING THE VISION

As stated in previous chapters, the leader must clearly explain the team's vision to the members. Without a clear vision, team members will not know what they need to do to meet their objectives. They need to understand how their actions will influence the team's vision.

Not everyone on the team will interpret what is said about the vision the same way. The leader should take into consideration team members' experience, knowledge, and backgrounds when conveying the vision. The key is to keep asking team members questions to be sure they understand what they need to do.

Leaders who share in the team vision by taking on their share of tasks lead by example and give their team members a clearer picture of what they should do. As the team becomes productive and sees results, the vision comes into perspective for them.

Effective leaders help to keep the vision in the team members' minds until the vision has been realized. Encourage the whole team to share and keep sharing the vision.

Tips for Leaders

- ◆ Clearly convey the team vision and goals.
- ◆ Be accessible.
- ◆ Communicate effectively.
- ◆ Lead by example.
- ◆ Make decisions.
- ◆ Solve problems.
- ◆ Inspire team members.
- ◆ Work with team members.
- ◆ Produce quality work.
- ◆ Accomplish tasks.
- ◆ Mentor team members.
- ◆ Hold yourself accountable.
- ◆ Hold team members accountable.
- ◆ Value each team member.
- ◆ Acknowledge team members' contributions.

Exercise: Convey the Team's Vision

The next time you lead a team, think about how you will clearly convey the team's vision. List ways you can help team members interpret the vision correctly, and help them do their part to realize that vision.

_____

_____

_____

_____

_____

_____

7 Making Group Decisions and Negotiating

Whenever a group of people is involved in the decision-making process, you can expect a discussion about which of their suggestions is the best solution to implement. This discussion may become quite spirited, but a solid debate of the pros and cons of an issue can be valuable in arriving at the optimum decision.

Do not assume there is one answer to the problems facing the team or one way of doing the tasks necessary to reach team goals. Each team member may have a different viewpoint on the issue at hand, and each may have an opinion on how to handle it. This diversity can have a positive effect on the team if members are willing to accept different views and to negotiate and compromise.

BUILDING TRUST

Trust is an absolute must for teams. All members must trust one another for the team to be successful. A culture of deceit and mistrust quickly undermines a team and its ability to meet goals. Team members must not only be trustworthy themselves but also be able to trust everyone else on the team.

You must earn team members' trust; you cannot force it on them. If you come right out and say, "Trust me," you run the risk of raising your teammates' suspicions. Demonstrate through your actions you can be trusted and are reliable. If you say you will do something, do it. If you have the slightest doubt you can accomplish what is asked of you, do not promise to do it. Once you break your word, you damage trust, and it is difficult to recover it.

Always do what is right regardless of personal drawbacks. Tell the truth; if you do not know an answer, admit it. If you have to deliver bad news to the team, do not lie or try to hide information. Be upfront and honest. You might feel that shielding teammates from bad news does them a favor by not upsetting them, but you erode their trust in you. They may make their own assumptions about what they think is really going on. This leads to idle and incorrect gossip.

Capable leaders and team members inspire trust and confidence. Set a positive example by doing your best at all times. Use good judgment, and contribute to the team goals. Set priorities and act on them.

Demonstrate you know how to work competently with teammates and you support the team leader. If you are the leader, take on the added responsibility of managing the team. Display competence.

Treat team members well. Let them know you have their interests in mind. Focus on your shared goals, and do what you can to help them with their tasks. Bring out the best in others, and appreciate their success and contributions toward the team's vision.

Be consistent in your actions. Use integrity in every situation—no exceptions. You cannot expect people to trust you if only act honorable some of the time.

Ways to foster team trust include, but are not limited to, the following:

- Keeping the lines of communication open
- Being trustworthy all the time
- Thinking the best of others
- Showing others you care
- Performing your work to the best of your ability
- Staying on task
- Meeting goal deadlines
- Taking credit only when due you
- Being competent
- Owning up to your shortcomings
- Acknowledging others' efforts and success
- Setting an example
- Being accessible
- Supporting your teammates

Exercise: Assess Trustworthiness

Think about the last time you were on a team. Do you feel your teammates trusted you and your abilities? Why or why not?

_____

_____

_____

_____

Think about the last time you were on a team. Did you trust your teammates and their abilities? Why or why not?

_____

_____

_____

_____

BUILDING RAPPORT

Developing a positive connection with team members is crucial to working together and setting the tone for a working relationship. To be effective, the leader must build a rapport with each team member. Team members should build a connection with each other.

Effective communication skills are essential for building rapport. Listen attentively; pay attention to the meaning behind the speaker's words. For example, you can tell a lot from someone's tone, her unorganized thoughts, or her evasion when giving answers. Encourage teammates to communicate openly with you.

Be friendly and approachable; look for common interests. It is difficult to work with people you hardly know. Find something you like about each team member and capitalize on that. Share information about yourself with them to encourage camaraderie.

Avoid complaining and whining; do not express anger in negative ways such as yelling at team members.

Be aware of your behavior at all times, and treat others as you would like to be treated. Be patient and understanding. Give the impression you are always willing to help others.

Here are ways to build rapport:

◆ Actively listening to one another

◆ Withholding criticism unless it is tactful and constructive

◆ Being respectful of everyone and his time

◆ Avoiding behavior that hurts another team member

◆ Accepting diversity

◆ Apologizing when you make a mistake

- Showing you care
- Keeping a positive attitude
- Helping teammates
- Maintaining integrity at all times

Exercise: Build Rapport

The next time you are on a team, list ways you personally can build rapport with your teammates.

_____

_____

_____

_____

_____

_____

Tips for Building Rapport

Genuinely like people.	Compromise.
Include everyone.	Encourage others.
Show respect.	Criticize constructively.
Look for common ground.	Appreciate teammates' efforts.
Listen attentively.	Applaud teammates' success.
Share willingly.	Don't complain.

ACCEPTING ACCOUNTABILITY

Individuals on the team must hold themselves and others accountable for completing their assigned tasks if they are to meet the team goals.

Show up for meetings, be on time, and stay until the meetings are over. Be prepared with necessary information and materials. Make sure your assignments are complete and presented in a professional manner. Complete all your tasks.

Meet deadlines and exceed expectations. Tasks that are not performed efficiently reflect poorly on all teammates and on the team goals. Make to-do lists, and take appropriate steps to complete your designated tasks.

Give no excuses, and accept none from other teammates. Accountability applies to everyone all the time. Avoid passing the blame on anyone else for problems or mistakes. Do not attempt to cover up failures and errors. Admit mistakes, and look for ways to correct them.

Some people have an incorrect perception of how they are performing. They may feel they are doing the right thing and completing their jobs efficiently, but others may feel differently. Ask for feedback so you know if you are on the right track, and give constructive feedback to others.

Tackle problems head on and make the best decision you can. If the decision turns out to be wrong, accept the consequences and look for another option.

Complete the following checklist.

Accountability	Yes	No
I hold myself accountable for my actions.		
I complete my tasks efficiently.		
I meet all deadlines.		
I do not give excuses for incorrect decisions.		
I admit mistakes.		
I do not try to cover up my mistakes.		
I set goals and consistently work toward their attainment.		
I do my part to meet the team's goals and help my teammates meet those goals.		
I hold my teammates accountable for their actions.		

You should have answered yes to each item in the checklist. Work toward correcting any negative answers.

Exercise: Assess Your Accountability

How do you hold yourself accountable for completing your tasks and meeting the organization's goals?

_____

_____

_____

_____

NEGOTIATING WITH THE TEAM

Negotiating is a key skill that all team members must utilize. Collaboration is necessary to reach the team goals, and it sometimes requires negotiating to reach solutions.

Individuals with different values and interests must find ways to work together to reach the team's goals. It is not always a smooth process when the team is extremely diverse. However, the team's diversity is also a strong point when it comes to generating ideas.

Passive members may go along with more forceful members. This is a mistake that prevents the team from working at optimum levels. Try to involve everyone on the team in contributing ideas and making decisions.

Team members must keep an open mind and work from the perspective that everything is negotiable and workable. The key is to find a way to come together and make decisions that benefit the team.

There is not always a clear winner or loser in a negotiation. The purpose of negotiating is to reach some kind of agreement that satisfies and benefits the members.

Negotiation Tips

- ◆ Listen attentively.
- ◆ Consider all points of view.
- ◆ Keep an open mind.
- ◆ Use positive language.
- ◆ Compromise.

- ◆ Do not use manipulation.
- ◆ Look for an amicable solution.
- ◆ Consider all parties' interests.
- ◆ Be objective.

Complete the following checklist.

Checklist for Negotiating	Yes	No
I am willing to compromise for the good of the team.		
I consider all suggestions when making decisions that affect the team.		
I look for the solution that benefits everyone on the team to some extent.		
I have a positive attitude and use positive language when discussing issues with the team.		
I do not manipulate team members in any way.		
I am objective.		
I am flexible in my thinking.		
I listen.		
I consider my words carefully before speaking.		
I hold myself accountable for my choices.		
I avoid making snap judgments.		

You should have answered yes to each item in the checklist. Work toward correcting any negative answers.

Tips for Making Decisions

◆ Define the problem.

◆ Analyze the problem.

◆ Make a list of possible solutions.

◆ Assess and choose the best option.

◆ Implement the solution.

◆ Evaluate the results of the solution.

◆ If the solution does not work, implement another one.

◆ Re-evaluate the results.

Exercise: Assess the Team's Negotiation Skills

The next time you are on a team, make note of how individual team members negotiate and compromise when arriving at decisions.

_____

_____

_____

_____

Exercise: Assess Your Negotiation Skills

List your personal traits that you feel benefit you when you need to compromise with team members or need to negotiate a solution that everyone can live with.

_____

_____

_____

_____

List your personal traits that you feel hinder you when you need to compromise with team members or need to negotiate a solution that everyone can live with. List ways to improve these negative traits.

_____

_____

_____

_____

8 Solving Problems

Team members are tasked with solving problems and attaining team goals. That's why it's crucial that they find ways to agree on issues that arise during their pursuit. Individuals who do not respect or value the contributions of other team members become a liability.

The best problem-solving solutions meet the needs of all team members. These solutions must be tied to the team's goals and vision.

IDENTIFYING PROBLEMS

The first step in solving problems is to identify them. That may seem obvious, but what is not so obvious is the true nature of the problem. The person who created the team might believe the problem is one thing, but the team may discover that is not the case. There may be underlying causes disguised by the so-called problem. For instance, the problem might be defined as unhappy customers because of poor customer service. The team organizer may feel the customer service representatives are providing poor service. However, by digging deeper, the team may discover that customers are unhappy because of poor access to customer service personnel, not because the personnel they do reach have provided poor service.

Generally, the team's problems are defined by the person who organized the team. After all, teams are created to solve problems. The team may have one or more problems to address and is tasked with identifying these problems and the issues surrounding them.

Once the issues have been identified, the team should select one problem at a time to work on. Working on too many problems at once may weaken the team's efficiency and productivity. Therefore, the team should examine all the problems, evaluate why they are obstacles to attaining the team's goals, prioritize the order in which to undertake the problems, and begin the search for appropriate solutions.

Ask questions such as these of each problem:

+ How important to attaining the team's goals is the solving of this problem in relation to the other problems?
+ Does the team have adequate resources to solve this problem?
+ What is the timeframe for solving this problem?
+ Can an individual team member solve this problem, or do all team members need to be involved?
+ Does this problem have underlying issues?
+ If the problem has underlying issues, what are they?
+ How much research is needed to solve this problem?
+ What are the consequences of not solving this problem?

Once you have asked these or similar questions about each problem, rank the problems in priority order according to the answers you have uncovered. Begin with the most important problem and work your way through the list.

ANALYZING PROBLEMS

Analyze the problem by asking *what, why, where, when*, and *how* questions. Find as much information as possible. Search for underlying issues. What you think is the problem may turn out to be a symptom of some other issue that turns out to be the real problem.

Strive to obtain complete, accurate information while analyzing the problem. Missing and incorrect facts impair the team's judgment. Be discerning. If possible, gather information from experts in the field rather than opinionated individuals.

We make decisions every day, and many of the decisions that team members face when trying to reach the team's goals are ones they typically encounter daily or weekly in the organization. An effective plan for analyzing and prioritizing problems increases the chances of coming up with viable solutions. The team's decision could still turn out to be a disappointment, but without a plan, the team is off to a poor start.

Begin by taking a hard, long look at the problem. Define it. Examine it from all angles, and put it in perspective. What is known about the problem? What do you still need to know about it? Are you sure what you are looking at is the real problem, or is there an underlying cause that is the true problem?

Exercise: Analyze Your Problem-Solving Skills

Analyze a time you were on a team and solved a problem successfully. Why do you feel you were successful?

_____

_____

_____

_____

_____

What steps did you take to solve the problem?

_____

_____

_____

_____

_____

THINKING CRITICALLY

Critical thinking is an approach to problem solving that involves asking questions and analyzing the answers. Critical thinkers are open-minded and willing to accept different viewpoints from theirs if it adds vital information they can use to solve problems.

Questions you can ask yourself when attempting to solve problems include these:

- ✦ What is the problem?
- ✦ Have I asked _who, what, when, where, why,_ and _how_ questions about the problem?
- ✦ What are all the facts surrounding the problem?
- ✦ Are all the relevant facts presented?
- ✦ What approach should I take to analyze the problem?
- ✦ What is the root cause of the problem?
- ✦ What is the logical approach to solving the problem?
- ✦ Have I brainstormed ideas?
- ✦ What are the best strategies to use to solve the problem?
- ✦ What is the logical conclusion for solving the problem?
- ✦ How will I handle obstacles to solving the problem?
- ✦ Can anyone else help me solve this problem?
- ✦ If I take the action I believe is best and it fails, what will I try next?

When thinking about the answers to the above questions, understand why the information you gather is important to the team's ability to solve the problem. Why should the team members care? Tell them.

As mentioned earlier in this chapter, team members may have differing viewpoints, and they should be regarded with a tolerant mind. Let go of the temptation to disregard ideas that differ from yours. Be tolerant of your teammates' opinions. Pursue the most logical solutions.

Make sure you have all the facts and they are presented accurately. Is there information to back up the facts? Are the sources used to gather information reputable? Reserve judgment until you are sure you have thought of everything.

Generate as many ideas as possible. Organize them, and separate the good ones from the useless ones. Examine and take apart the facts. Do they seem sound? Out of all the possible ideas, determine which is most logical or reasonable. Be sure to consider the time, manpower, and resources an idea will take to implement.

Accept that you will face obstacles and that not all your decisions will work out the way you hope they will. If you have a setback, put it in the proper frame. In addition, there may be conflict among team members because of strong differences of opinions. Find a way to work together, keeping the team's goals in mind. Chapter 9, "Handling Conflict," provides tips for getting along with the team.

Exercise: Assess Critical Thinking Skills

Think about the last time you were on a team. Did you use critical-thinking skills? If not, why not? If you did, what was the process?

_____

_____

_____

_____

_____

CREATING SOLUTIONS

Break down complex problems into manageable parts. Staring at a huge, complicated issue can be intimidating. Therefore, suspend judgment and seek creative solutions. Do not take things for granted and base decisions on old assumptions. For example, if a client accepted a solution for late shipments in the past, it does not hold that he will accept the same results a second time. Analyze the information you have, add what you know to it, and seek new information from your teammates and credible outside sources.

After gathering all the facts and analyzing them, think about possible steps you can take to resolve the situation. Brainstorm ideas, request the help you need, and do your research. Once you are confident you have arrived at the most logical steps to take, implement them. Assess the situation after implementing your decision to determine if it was successful. If it was not, go back to your brainstorm ideas and choose another one to implement. Assess it to see if it worked. Continue the process until the problem is resolved or you have exhausted your ideas.

Because teams are organized to solve problems, the team members must always be working toward solutions. Not all solutions are acceptable to every member. The best scenario is to come to an agreement everyone can live with that still meets the goals of the team. The quicker team members reach accord, the quicker they can meet the goals. That is not to say team members should be too hasty or that any team member should be coerced into reaching an agreement.

When team members reflect on a possible solution, they must consider whether the solution will be acceptable to the person who organized the team and to the organization as a whole. The team may be in agreement, but the organization might veto it. Consider the following:

✦ Look for solutions in which all team members benefit.

✦ Consider possible solutions from every angle.

✦ Be sure the organization will approve the situation.

✦ Look for miscalculations and oversights in the solution.

✦ Consider the implications of implementing the solution.

Complete the following checklist.

Checklist for Creating Solutions	Yes	No
I am open-minded when considering solutions.		
I have looked at the problem from all angles.		
I have brainstormed ideas.		
I have gathered information from experts.		
I have considered the benefits of the solution to all team members.		
I believe the solution is the best one available.		
I believe the organization will approve of the solution.		
I have considered the implications of implementing the solution.		

You should have answered yes to each item in the checklist. Work toward correcting any negative answers.

Exercise: Analyze Solutions

Think of a time you were on a team. What was the procedure used to develop solutions to problems?

_____

_____

_____

_____

What issues do you believe should be considered when seeking solutions to team problems?

_____

_____

_____

_____

DETERMINING THE APPROPRIATE SOLUTION

Team members should discuss the proposed solutions, take a look at all the pros and cons, and decide the criteria they will use to arrive at a decision. They should then select the solution that is best for the situation and for the team by asking these questions:

✦ Is this the best solution?

✦ Is this the most cost- and time-effective solution?

✦ Will this solution benefit the organization the most?

✦ Will this solution be permanent, or is it likely the same problem will resurface?

✦ How easy will it be to implement the solution?

✦ Who will implement the solution?

✦ Will this solution likely cause other problems?

The team must be certain the proposed solution meets with the organization's approval. The team members will be held accountable for its success or failure.

Exercise: Determine a Solution

Think of a time you were on a team. Was the team successful in arriving at a solution to the problems it was tasked to resolve? Why or why not?

_____

_____

_____

_____

IMPLEMENTING THE SOLUTION

Once the solution is decided, the team will advise the person who called for the creation of the team or other organization official. The proper individuals should then implement the solution. The team should ask if they should execute the solution or if someone outside the team will do it. The solution must be monitored to determine if it succeeds in solving the problem.

If the solution appears to be working, the team should determine if it was effective and efficient and whether it is a permanent fix.

If the solution does not work, the team should go back and reanalyze the problem, discuss other possible solutions, and try something else.

Exercise: Implement a Solution

Think of a time you were on a team and the team implemented a solution to the problems it was tasked to resolve. Was the solution successful? Why or why not?

_____

_____

_____

_____

_____

_____

9 Handling Conflict

When a number of divergent personalities work together, conflict may arise. Not all team members agree all the time. However, not all disagreements are unhealthy when it comes to reaching team goals. Sometimes discussions produce optimal results because people are forced to rethink their views and consider those of teammates. Drawing from various experts and their viewpoints, knowledge, and interests can be beneficial to the team. It is when these differences turn into fights and negative encounters that conflict becomes detrimental to the team and must be stopped.

The team leader must continually monitor team members and deal with unconstructive conflicts as soon as they arise. Having policies in place to handle problem behavior aids the leader in deciding when to step in and how to deal with the conflict.

IDENTIFYING SOURCES OF CONFLICT

At the first meeting, team members should identify potential conflicts and decide how to handle them. This information is then written down in the policies and procedures for the team.

Potential conflicts may include but are not limited to the following:

- ✦ Biases
- ✦ Incompetence
- ✦ An incompetent member taking over
- ✦ Bossy team members
- ✦ Negative personalities
- ✦ Too many diverse personalities
- ✦ Closed minds
- ✦ Team members believing they are not given credit
- ✦ Team members believing too much credit is given to someone else
- ✦ Unproductive meetings
- ✦ Unreasonable deadlines
- ✦ Strong personal opinions

Conflict arising from anger or other negative behavior should concern the leader and the team members. This type of conflict can deteriorate into a damaging situation if left unchecked. Having the team's procedures for handling disruptive and unproductive team members in place and following those procedures encourages team members to behave properly. If an unruly team member refuses to amend his behavior, removal from the team may be the only recourse.

Good team players can become embroiled in conflicts. Why? Differences of opinions, misunderstandings, approaching deadlines, divergent viewpoints, and many other issues can cause conflicts. Conflicts can become problems if the team cannot work through them or if they affect the team's achieving its goals.

Many team members take it personally when others do not agree with their ideas or solutions. The leader needs to find a way to move those team members away from insisting on their solution being the right and fair one to finding a solution everyone can agree to implement. The leader might point out the pros and cons of each solution presented. If the team still cannot agree, the leader may have to be the final vote.

The way team members perceive a situation often leads to conflict. Some members may believe another is getting credit they do not deserve. Another member may feel she has not been properly recognized for outstanding work. Someone may feel his idea was rejected because another team member does not like him.

Exercise: Determine Sources of Conflict

Think about a time you were on a team. What are some sources of conflict the team experienced?

_____

_____

_____

_____

_____

MANAGING CONFLICT

Many people are uncomfortable dealing with conflict, but as soon as quarrels arise, the leader or person monitoring the team should dispense the consequences according to the established team policies. Arguments left unchecked can turn into bitter debates. Dealing with abusively argumentative team members can destroy the team or defeat its members.

Some conflicts are not worth bothering about because they are inconsequential or the team has more pressing issues with which to deal. In such cases, urge team members to move on to the next issue.

Keep in mind that not all conflict is angry conflict. Sometimes it is simply a case of team members expressing their opinions and views. That type of discussion can lead to a well-rounded analysis of ideas.

If you are the team leader, prepare before tackling team conflicts. Find out the main problem and its underlying issues, gather related information, consider the members involved in the conflict, and formulate a plan of action. Ask yourself the following questions or ones that will help you decide how to handle the conflict:

- How important is the issue at the center of the conflict?
- Is there a way to contain the conflict?
- Am I prepared to handle the conflict?
- How can I get team members to come to agreement?
- Should I implement the team procedures for handling conflicts?
- Am I able to control my emotions regarding the conflict?
- If I cannot control my own emotions about the situation, can I ask another teammate to step in?
- What can I do to keep the conflict from disrupting the team's goal achievement?
- Do I have authority to settle the conflict?
- Can someone else settle the conflict?

Team members must learn to deal with conflicts in a professional manner and avoid turning disagreements into obstacles to success.

To make sure you are not contributing to team conflicts, overcome the urge to join in the complaining, and avoid arguing. If discussions get out of hand, step back and compose yourself, and ask your teammates to do the same.

Tips for Dealing with Conflict

- Remain calm during discussions.	- Cooperate.
- Listen to teammates.	- Do not be judgmental.
- Let go of the need to be right.	- Do not discriminate or show bias.
- Be courteous.	- Be patient.
- Look at things from your teammates' point of view.	- Avoid jumping to conclusions.
- Be tactful.	- Remain in control of emotions.

Complete the following checklist.

Checklist for Handling Conflict	Yes	No
I remain calm and professional during team discussions.		
I am cooperative.		
I reserve judgment until I have all the facts.		
I consider my teammates' point of view.		
I do not jump to conclusions.		
I do not argue with angry team members.		
I criticize positively.		
I negotiate to find solutions that work for everyone.		

You should have answered yes to each item in the checklist. Work toward correcting any negative answers.

Exercise: Analyze Team Discussions

Think about a time you were on a team and members discussed solutions to problems. Answer the following questions:

How did the team handle conflicts?_____

_____

_____

_____

Who on the team was rude and highly argumentative? _____

How did the team deal with this person?_____

_____

_____

_____

Who on the team were the peacemakers? _____

How did they go about keeping the peace? _____

_____

_____

_____

PASSING BLAME

Situations are never clear and predictable when working with others. When the team fails to reach its goals, the leader and the members seek someone or something to blame. But this reproach does nothing to solve the problem. A better tactic is to find a way to overcome the obstacles and move toward the goals.

Team members may cast blame for a number of reasons, including their belief that some members did not do their part, guidelines were unclear, meetings were a waste of time, leadership was poor, resources were scarce or unavailable, deadlines were too tight, and on and on. Those members who are blamed for not performing satisfactorily in turn defend themselves and their actions. This blame game leads to conflicts but does little to help the team attain its goals. A successful team gets past the censuring and figures out how to resolve the situation.

To lessen the prospect of passing blame, the team designs procedures to interrupt poor performance before it compromises the team's goals. Guidelines should be clearly defined, and team members should be given clear directives regarding their duties. They should be asked to restate the directions to be sure they understand what is required of them. Meetings should be run efficiently, and all members should report on time and be prepared. Without exception, ill-prepared members should be dealt with according to the team's policies and procedures.

Who or what is to blame for the team's failure to reach its goals? Listed next are a number of possible causes for a team's failure:

- ✦ Team members do not complete tasks.
- ✦ Team members do not perform up to standards.
- ✦ Team members argue excessively.
- ✦ An incompetent team member tries to take over.
- ✦ Resources are lacking.
- ✦ There's insufficient time to complete tasks.
- ✦ Directions are unclear.
- ✦ Interpretation of directions is incorrect.
- ✦ Leadership is inadequate.
- ✦ Team members have poor skills.
- ✦ Meetings are mismanaged.
- ✦ Some team members have personality conflicts.

Exercise: Assess Who Is to Blame

Think about a time you were on a team when a discussion turned into a blame game. What was the outcome of the situation?

_____

_____

_____

Can you think of a way the situation could have been handled better?

_____

_____

_____

Exercise: Win Over Team Members

The next time you are on a team, think about how you can convince members to stop passing the blame and complete their tasks. Write down your ideas.

_____

_____

_____

_____

COLLABORATING

A team member's personality traits greatly affect team performance by influencing the other members. Positive personality traits such as a cooperative attitude, open-mindedness, and tolerance tend to increase the team's cohesiveness and productivity. Negative traits such as poor morale, bias, and antisocial behavior create a problematic atmosphere.

An ideal team would be composed of members whose personalities complement one another. Even in this case, conflict is a possibility. Team members will be engaged in multiple discussions during their time together, and these discussions may lead to disagreements that turn into clashes of wills and arguments.

The team leader should monitor the progress of the team, including everyone's ability to get along with one another. Individuals who display negative habits and problematic attitudes should be taken aside and reminded of the team's policies and the consequences of not abiding by them.

Team members who are controlling and consistently try to take over when they have not been assigned a leadership role can be the source of conflict and stress. The team leader should arrest the behavior of these team members immediately, or they may become completely out of control and detrimental to the team.

Team members who feel they are being taken advantage of or that they are doing more work than others on the team may become disenchanted and evade their responsibilities. The leader should make all team members feel they are important to the team and their responsibilities are best suited to the tasks they are assigned. Not all team members will have equal responsibilities because of their particular skills and expertise. That said, the leader should try to balance the responsibilities and duties among the team members.

Oftentimes the best strategy for collaborating is for team members to compromise. If the team has spent enough time debating an issue that will not particularly obstruct the goal, the leader might choose a resolution. The leader may also call for moving past the issue or revisiting it whenever more information has been gathered.

Exercise: Collaborate with Team Members

Write down the ways in which you positively collaborate with team members.

_____

_____

_____

_____

_____

USING DEMOGRAPHICS

Team demographics may influence the compatibility of the group. Teams composed of members who have similar interests because of their backgrounds may have better communication and unity among members. Individuals with divergent experiences may become embroiled in persistent conflicts. For instance, a team made up of a majority of individuals in their twenties and a couple of people in their fifties will have very different views. The older, experienced team members may have a difficult time relating to the younger members if they insist on dramatic changes to the status quo. The younger members may feel the older ones are out of touch.

When the demographics of the team correlate, the members have a greater likelihood of unifying and of achieving their goals.

Exercise: Analyze Team Demographics

The next time you are on a team, observe the team's demographics and record how you believe those demographics will serve the team well.

_____

_____

_____

_____

_____

The next time you are on a team, observe the team's demographics and record how you believe those demographics will hinder the team.

_____

_____

_____

_____

ADDRESSING THE PROBLEMS

As a rule, people have tendencies to exaggerate, blame others, defend themselves, misunderstand, stick to their opinions, and the like. Given these issues, there is little wonder that conflict arises among team members.

All issues and conflicts must be promptly addressed to increase cohesiveness among team members and help them reach their goals. When members are preoccupied with upheaval and arguments, their performance and efforts toward reaching team goals are adversely affected. When emotions run high, productivity and commitment drop.

The first thing the team leader must do is gather complete, accurate information about the conflict. It is imperative that she has the full picture to address the problems properly. She should ask questions rather than demand compliance, choose words carefully when looking for answers, and be sensitive to team members' feelings.

Individual members may have different notions of what is expected of them. The leader needs to clarify why there is a discrepancy between the performance and the requirements. Individuals may feel they are justified in their behavior, but the leader needs to clarify acceptable behavior according to the team's policies.

Help create a climate in which team members feel free to discuss their opinions and ideas without being afraid of repercussions. Let them know you are willing to listen to them and that it is not all right to intimidate their teammates.

Exercise: Assess the Team Leader

Think about a time you worked on a successful team. How did the leader contribute to the team's success?

_____

_____

_____

_____

How did your teammates contribute to the team's success?

_____

_____

_____

How did you contribute to the team's success?

_____

_____

_____

10 Empowering Teams

Team members may perform their tasks more efficiently if they are empowered to carry out the goals of the team without having to check in with the leader every step of the way. Before being empowered, team members must have clear direction and knowledge of what they are supposed to do. Therefore, one of the most important steps to empowering the team is to provide them with what they need.

Empowered team members who are given the opportunity to manage themselves and their tasks are excited to put their ideas into practice. They often cannot wait to see how their suggestions help the team and what new ideas they can envision. Without empowerment, team members will do what they are told but seldom go out of their way to make suggestions or try new methods and techniques, especially if they feel no one is listening to them.

ESTABLISHING AN ENVIRONMENT FOR SUCCESS

Chapter 4, "Considering Culture, Competence, Cooperation, and Communication," and Chapter 7, "Making Group Decisions and Negotiating," stress the importance of open communication, trust, and making decisions. All these things contribute to empowerment, and a lack of them hampers team members from believing they should take the risks sometimes necessary to reach their goals. Team members who understand the vision, the purpose for their assigned tasks, their roles, and the direction in which they should proceed will be able to take appropriate action on their own.

Leaders should provide the means for team members to communicate freely at any point. By setting up regular meetings and letting team members know they can approach them anytime, leaders make team members feel they are being taken seriously. These leaders also offer the chance for team members to clarify issues that confuse them, seek help with problems, and advise of progress.

When team members come to the leader with a problem, the leader should not immediately solve it for them but rather give the members the opportunity to figure it out. For instance, the leader may ask the team members what they think is the best way to handle the situation or may generate a discussion among the members.

Chapter 3, "Setting Team Roles and Goals," stresses the importance of making sure team members understand their roles and the roles of their teammates. How can the team members know what they can and cannot do if they do not have clearly defined roles? They need to know the requirements and limitations of their roles so they perform as expected but do not overstep their positions and infringe on a teammate's responsibilities.

Exercise: Assess the Team Environment

Think about a time you worked on a successful team. Did you feel the environment was conducive to success? Why or why not?

_____

_____

_____

_____

_____

LEADING THE EMPOWERED TEAM

The leader who hopes to empower team members must clearly describe the team's vision and convey all information the team needs to reach its goals. Otherwise, the team does not know what it is working toward. The leader or the team members may then define the team roles and responsibilities and prepare to make the best decisions.

When team members know what is expected of them and how to do it, they spend less time second-guessing themselves and agonizing over whether they are performing their tasks correctly and to the organization's standards. They can concentrate on doing their jobs.

In addition to conveying the team's vision and associated information, the leader should impart whatever expertise and knowledge she personally has that can assist the team. Sharing expertise helps the members grow and become more productive in reaching their goals.

Effective team leaders do not tell the team members what to do. Instead, the leader asks the right questions to determine what kind of help the team members need or steer them in the right direction. The leader also encourages team members and influences them in a way that helps them succeed.

Leaders must be good listeners and give team members their full attention when they come to them by making eye contact, asking pertinent questions, and restating what they heard. They should take team members' ideas under serious consideration. Team members whose ideas are constantly rejected may come to feel it is useless to tell the leader anything. These members stop contributing ideas, and a creative path is lost. Even if a team member's idea cannot be used, credit should be given for suggesting it.

Members of empowered teams have a hand in setting the team's goals and individual members' goals, and they determine the steps to take to attain the goals instead of having that information dictated to them by the leader or the organization. Once they understand why the team was created, team members can decide how to operate as a team to achieve their goals. Empowered members are inclined to work up to their ability and even push themselves further than they did in the past because they now have a say in how they perform their tasks.

Some empowered teams choose their own leaders who then organize and monitor the team's activities. These leaders might guide members and facilitate meetings, but they do not make decisions for the team members. Leaders of empowered teams do not micromanage or control or tell individuals how to perform their tasks.

In other empowered teams, the members are all leaders, or they rotate in the leadership position. In such teams, the organization must clearly convey the vision and purpose of the team and the authority that the team members possess.

Leaders who empower the team do the following:

+ Clearly describe the team's vision and how it contributes to the organization.
+ Openly communicate information team members need.
+ Urge team members to take responsibility for determining what roles they will fill.
+ Encourage team members to schedule their own tasks and set their own goals.
+ Mentor team members.
+ Care about team members.
+ Motivate the team.
+ Encourage the team.
+ Convey the parameters in which the team members can operate.
+ Inspire team members to take reasonable risks.
+ Avoid micromanaging the team members.
+ Provide feedback.
+ Free team members to use their talents.
+ Make it easier for team members to reach their goals.
+ Let every team member know he is important to the team.
+ Expect team members to hold themselves and other members accountable.

Empowering the team members does not mean the leader is detached from the team. Team leaders who empower team members must stay informed of what is happening. They continue to supply adequate resources and make the tough decisions when the team is stalled.

Exercise: Assess the Team Leadership

Think about a time you worked on a successful team. Did you feel the team leader empowered you and other team members? Why or why not?

_____

_____

_____

_____

ENERGIZING TEAM MEMBERS

Empowered team members seem to have more energy and enthusiasm than those who are directed by authoritarian leaders. When people are given the freedom to pursue their duties as they see fit without interference from leaders, they often feel good about themselves and their accomplishments and become motivated and willing to contribute. Again, monitoring is necessary because some team members shirk their responsibilities.

Leaders can energize team members by giving them leeway to perform their tasks and avoiding constantly watching everything they do. They should encourage team members to try new things and use their imaginations. Team members will, hopefully, learn from their new responsibilities. Leaders who dictate and direct team members squelch their independence, self-confidence, and morale.

Encourage team members to try new things without being afraid of penalties if they fail. Let team members know you would rather they try and fail than not to exercise their creativity and problem-solving ability. Instruct them on how to take calculated risks.

Without constraints, team members are free to manage their own tasks and time. They can get as involved as they want and determine their own purpose for completing goals. Their tasks take on a greater importance to them. They often do higher-quality work out of a sense of pride. Team members put more care into their job performance and often have fun working on tasks.

Exercise: Assess the Team's Enthusiasm

Think about a time you worked on a successful team. Did you feel the team members were energized and enthusiastic? Why or why not?

_____

_____

_____

_____

_____

ASSESSING EMPOWERED TEAM MEMBERS

The leader should monitor the progress of team members once they are empowered and provide appropriate feedback. The leader should advise team members if they veer from the team's vision or its goals. Team members should be given the opportunity to correct the situation.

If the team fails to succeed because of the empowered team members' decisions, the leader should help them learn from the situation. Instead of blaming or reprimanding the team members, the leader should acknowledge their attempt to take risks. Hopefully, the team will grow from the experience and develop better judgment for the future.

Empowered team members are enthusiastic and want to make a positive impact. They seem to be energized by added responsibilities. Team members should support one another and work together to accomplish team goals.

Empowered team members develop many positive personal traits including, but not limited to, the following:

- Taking responsibility for their jobs
- Actively contributing to the team's vision and goals
- Enjoying their work
- Believing their work has meaning
- Making decisions themselves
- Controlling how they perform their tasks
- Being skilled and knowledgeable
- Energetically searching for solutions
- Being enthusiastic about their work
- Being more productive
- Rising to a challenge
- Handling a variety of tasks
- Monitoring their own performance
- Seeking feedback
- Wanting to make a positive impact on the team
- Taking calculated risks
- Believing in themselves
- Wanting to succeed
- Supporting coworkers and the team leader

If empowered team members feel they can do whatever they want and not answer to anyone, the leader must remind them of the boundaries and the consequences of not performing up to standards.

Complete the following checklist.

Checklist for Leaders to Empower the Team	Yes	No
I trust my team members to do a good job.		
I give my team members complete information regarding the team vision.		
I give my team members complete information regarding their assigned tasks.		
I give my team members complete information regarding their roles on the team.		
I encourage team members to use their creativity and problem-solving skills.		
I provide necessary training for the team.		
I provide feedback.		
I provide necessary resources.		
I let team members know how important their contributions are to the team and organization.		
I do not hover over my team members and watch their every move.		
I reward team members who have made valuable contributions to the team.		

You should have answered yes to each item in the checklist. Work toward correcting any negative answers.

Exercise: Empower the Team

Think about a time you were on a team. Do you feel you were empowered? Explain your answer.

_____

_____

_____

_____

The next time you are a team leader, think about how you can empower the team members. Write your answer here.

_____

_____

_____

_____

BUILDING SELF-ESTEEM

Leaders or the organization should reward team members who do a good job. This reward can take the form of money, extra time off, a letter of achievement, a new title, or any other form of recognition for a job well done. Valued team members are generally optimistic, productive, and committed. They have a positive influence on team morale.

A promotion can be a good self-esteem builder, but only if the team member is qualified and skilled enough to handle the new responsibilities. Organizations that provide skills training and personal development training to team members give them the expertise needed to do their jobs. Team members comfortable performing their tasks have higher self-esteem than those who feel inadequate or incompetent. The members who increase their knowledge base may also be apt to take more risks when performing tasks and making decisions. Create an environment where people are willing to grow and change.

Encouraging team members to try out their ideas and do things differently inspires them to break out of the old thoughts and fears that could be holding them back. Acknowledge and reward members who share with the team.

Employees should be encouraged to develop personal growth plans. The team leader is in a position to mentor members and help them devise these plans.

Complete the following checklist to determine if you are a leader who builds team members' self-esteem.

Building Self-Esteem	Yes	No
I let my team members know that I trust them to do a good job.		
I encourage team members to try new ways of doing tasks.		
I provide skills training for team members.		
I acknowledge excellent performance by team members.		
I encourage team members to create personal growth plans.		
I provide appropriate feedback.		
I keep the lines of communication open.		
I believe in my team members.		

You should have answered yes to each item in the checklist. Work toward correcting any negative answers.

Exercise: Build Self-Esteem

The next time you are on a team, observe how the leader builds or destroys team members' self-esteem. Write your observations here.

_____

_____

_____

_____

_____

The next time you are a team leader, develop a system for building team members' self-esteem. Write your ideas here.

_____

_____

_____

_____

_____

_____

11 Using Team Building Exercises

Many companies use team building exercises in an attempt to create cohesive teams that work well together. You can find many team building exercise books in stores and online. Companies specializing in team building activities come into your organization and organize appropriate activities.

Some team building exercises can be completed in the office, and others are performed outdoors. Many of the exercises are planned for weekend team building workshops. You may want to look for materials and exercises that fit your organization's needs.

Team building exercises are also effective for discovering team leaders. Many times during the completion of exercises, certain team members stand out from the group or take the lead in solving problems, finding information, and the like.

Why team building exercises? Here are some benefits of team building:

+ Introducing team members who have not previously met or worked together
+ Finding commonalities among team members
+ Building camaraderie
+ Urging team members to work together
+ Encouraging team members to trust one another
+ Discovering leaders

Exercise: Assess Team Building Exercises

Think about a time you were on a team. Did you do team building activities? If so, describe them here and state their effectiveness. If you did not do team building exercises, do you think they would have been valuable to the team?

_____

_____

_____

_____

USING ICEBREAKERS

Sometimes team leaders use team building exercises to introduce team members to one another. Many of these exercises are brief and fun. Icebreakers are a good way for team members to learn one another's names and to find something in common so they can form a cohesive group.

Many activities can be found in team building books and online. The following examples are brief icebreakers to help team members get to know each other.

Get Acquainted

Pair team members, and have them answer three questions about each other. Make at least one of the questions fun, such as, "What is your fondest memory?" Sample questions include these:

- ✦ What was your major in school?
- ✦ What project did you work on that you are most proud of?
- ✦ Whom do you admire most?
- ✦ What tasks do you enjoy performing the most?
- ✦ What was your proudest moment?
- ✦ What is your favorite thing to do?
- ✦ What kind of music do you listen to?
- ✦ Do you have a pet?
- ✦ What is your favorite food?
- ✦ What is something few people know about you?
- ✦ How far do you live from work?
- ✦ How did you get this job?
- ✦ What are your qualifications for being chosen for this team?

Set a time limit for answering the questions, and then have team members share the answers with the group.

Get the Facts

Pass around a thick pack of blank note cards, and ask team members to take as many cards as they think they will need, up to ten. Do not tell them what the note cards are for. After they have chosen their note cards, they must share a fact about themselves for each note card they took. For instance, if they took five note cards, they must share five facts with the team.

REENERGIZING TEAM MEMBERS

You can arrange exercises meant to reenergize team members who have worked on teams with each other before or who know each other fairly well. Team members could do a scavenger as described later in "Pitting Teams Against Each Other" or some of the exercises listed in this section.

Truth or Lie

Have team members write down two truths and one lie about themselves. Have a team member read her card. Ask the rest of the team members to decide which of the statements is a lie. Team members must come to an agreement. You may want to set a time limit so the discussions do not take up too much time.

Who Knew?

In advance of the team exercise, have each team member give you a fact about himself he does not think the other team members know. Type two lists on separate pieces of paper: one list of the team members' names, the other list of the facts you collected. At the team building exercise, pass out a copy of each list to the team members and have them pair the names with the little-known facts.

Whom Do You Admire?

Have each team member state whom she admires most and why.

PITTING TEAMS AGAINST EACH OTHER

Many team building exercises can be used to get multiple teams to interact with one another. Some of these exercises are for outdoors, such as having teams compete by rowing boats across a small lake or climbing a climbing wall. Other exercises can be done in the offices. The following examples are exercises that can be done with two or more teams.

Scavenger Hunt

Give each team a list of work-related items for which they have to search. Let them know the boundaries for the items, and set a time limit. When time is up, bring the team together to discuss how they went about locating the items.

A variation of this is to give each team a list of questions for which they have to find answers. Set a time limit. When time is up, bring the team together to discuss how they went about locating the items.

Circle of Facts

Have one team form a circle. Then have another team form a circle outside the first one. Have team members face each other, and give them one minute to find out something about each other. After a minute ring a bell. Ask everyone to move one person to the right and give the group a minute to find out something about that person. Continue in one-minute segments until everyone has had a chance to ask everyone else something about themselves.

Paired

Come up with a list of items that go together, such as dark and night, sun and moon, milk and cookies, peanut butter and jelly, and the like. Separate the pairs, and write one of them on a sheet of paper. Write the match on another sheet of paper; for example, write sun on one paper and moon on another.

Attach a piece of paper with one of the items from the pair to the back of each person and have each walk around asking yes or no questions to find his perfect match. Once team members find their match, they are to find out two things about the other person.

Shapes

Have different shapes drawn on sheets of paper, one shape to each sheet. Stand in front of the team members holding the shape so they cannot see it. Describe the shape to them and have them draw it from your verbal description.

Exercise: Choose Team Building Exercises

The next time you are on a team, arrange or suggest a team building exercise you feel would benefit the group.

_____

_____

_____

_____

Exercise: Build Stronger Teams

The next time you are on a team, research team building exercises you feel will help you and your coworkers become better team members. Choose an exercise, and make a list of reasons you think it would benefit you. Propose the exercise to your employer.

_____

_____

_____

_____

_____